ACROSS A DARKLING PLAIN

HARPER'S
MAGAZINE
PRESS

Other books by Marshall Frady
Wallace

Across a

Marshall Frady

Darkling Plain

An American's Passage Through the Middle East

A Harper's Magazine Press Book
Published in Association with Harper & Row
New York

I owe this book to my friend Willie Morris, whose notion it all was to begin with, and to my wife Gloria, who brought me through the writing of it.

CONTENTS

A Darkling Plain

ONLY FOUR DAYS ago, he had stepped onto this continent, into this hemisphere, for the first time in his life— emerging from the plane at the Cairo airport into a smoldering late afternoon swooning with a sweetness of flower beds. Now, still trying to grope out of the befuddlement that had lingered ever since that moment, he was being transported, this brilliant May morning three months before the cease-fire, to Suez, a medieval town lying on that long thin ultimate line to the east where two peoples, two orders, two languages were in some immense violent engagement: going there, himself, out of a simple dim instinct that only at the hot quick existential edge of mortal confrontation would the conflict finally define itself. His escort, a somewhat dumpy and morose girl from the Egyptian press ministry, exchanged occasional mutters with the Cairo cabdriver, but they rode for the most part in silence, spanking over a narrow rippled highway, across a vast pale haze of desert yawning off to dim prodigious mountains: a moonscape emptiness in which the only infiltrations of consciousness seemed at first to be merely a distant insectlike procession of high-tension towers, until, as they were nearing the front, he began to sense more than see tiny innumerable stirrings around them, hints across that immense blankness of some dense mute habitation, like an endless infestation of trap-door spiders or prairie dogs, and at last he realized they had been moving for several miles now through the midst of an army.

When they entered Suez, it was like some city of the plague, empty and mustard yellow in the shadeless still glare of high noon; an astonishing labyrinth of wreckage, with windows in pocked and bitten walls through which he could see sunlight on fallen rafters, the only sound in its streets now the far loonlike hooting of a bird. It was as if there had occurred here some monstrous event of vandalism, a mad night of systematic breakage and trampling still inexplicable to the few people trickling among it now in the daylight. They finally stopped at the edge of the Gulf of Suez, the cars bearing the other foreign reporters pulling up behind them, and as he got out he saw, across the chalk-blue water, the long quiet shoreline of a last spit of land, a low indistinct blur of sand and green that faced the Canal: the other side.

Then, while they were all gathered in a bunker, listening to a briefing with electric fans whispering over their heads and dainty glasses of hot sweet tea being passed around, they began to hear the dull distant whumps of another bombing raid. Venturing back outside, they found the empty streets now filled with the sound of a faint ghostly rushing. The planes were too high to see. But under that crisscrossing of invisible whines in the blue blank sky, the gutted blocks of Suez seemed suspended in a curious hush, with only a pretty twittering of birds among the rubble, the occasional stuttering clumps of detonations from somewhere on the outskirts of town. They wandered on for a distance, peering up now and then at the sky, past the toppled walls of courtyards, turning at one corner where, over the vacant boarded hulk of a movie theatre, an old poster—five women and a prostrate man in some gleeful gaudy pornographic romp now weather-paled and fading—fluttered soundlessly from the marquee in a soft Gulf wind. A television crew walking down the exact center of the street ahead of him called to each other occasionally, their voices seeming in the silence to ring for blocks around them, and he suddenly had the impression that, passing around another corner, they would vanish, simply be translated into the very air. Strolling finally into the courtyard of a hospital that was still in operation, the journalists were presently greeted by a surgeon in a pale green gown who lit a cigarette with fingertips stained a dim red. As he was talking to them, another jet's thin machined moan passed high overhead, and the surgeon and his staff instantly retreated back against the hospital wall.

For some minutes now, he had been feeling an impulse to blurt, *Just what the hell—what the hell is going on here?* Those leisurely looping whines in the sky, the remote bumps in the quiet bright noon seemed abstract, unconnected to the tremendous violence around them that they had all been brought here to behold; some final truth, some secret, had escaped the bunker recital of technical statistics and tabulations. At last, as they were making their way back to the cars, the high long wails faded from the sky, and after a tentative silence of some fifteen minutes a few people began ebbing back out from unsuspected crannies, quickly and obliviously resuming along a sleazy back street their meager trade in onions and tomatoes and bread and coffee, in a sunshine which yet seemed to glisten with some strange fatality. Presently, a woman like an ageless gnome, wrapped in black cloth from her head to her bare ankles, materialized among the wooden carts, swaggering slowly with extravagant pumps of her hips down the aisle formed for her by the few male inhabitants still left in town—soldiers and peddlers—she cawing and whooping to them as she distributed along her way little upward-pinching gestures of one hand: the indestructible Rose of Suez.

Finally, before they reached the cars, a television correspondent struck a pose with his microphone atop a heap of debris and inquired of his cameraman, "Can't we wait for some more planes to come over?" and when his cameraman assured him the raid was over for the day and they could overlay the sounds caught earlier on their tape, the correspondent braced himself with a deep breath, the camera began to hum, and after one long significant gaze heavenward, he began to intone, "The planes . . . you hear above me now . . . are Israeli planes. . . ."

He rode back to Cairo with two other Americans, one of them a woman of somewhat anonymous origin and obscure function. Turned out breezily in slacks and sweater and scarf as if for a pleasant morning's outing to a suburban shopping center, her face still fresh and glad-eyed against only the faintest first blurrings of age, she merely allowed, in a voice with the invincibly cheerful accents of the Midwest, that she had taught school somewhere in Colorado and was on an information-gathering excursion through the Arab lands, alighting when she could at the homes of former students. During the bombing back in Suez, she had sent a soldier out from the bunker to hold her tape recorder up toward the sky for a few minutes while she watched him from the entranceway, and now, on the way back to Cairo, she replayed the tape. "You can hear them flying," she chimed. "Listen. There goes one. But you weren't able to see them, were you? I had really hoped to get a snapshot of one of them flying over. Listen—there's another one. But it doesn't seem I got any of the booms, when the bombs were hitting; all you can do is hear them flying. You can't hear any booms. Hey, wait a minute—there was one. Oh, good. I got a boom. . . ." Sometime after he had left Egypt, while he was standing with other journalists at a guard post in Jordan waiting for clearance to go on down to the river, a car pulled up beside them and she suddenly bloomed forth from its back door, still resolutely spangle-eyed and earnest, blithe in a powder-blue chiffon smock and a matching hairband, only now she had, dangling from a cord around her neck, a single plump oily bullet. When he asked her how she had come by that memento, she paused for an instant with a slightly accosted smile on her face, then blinked once in the pitiless sunlight and answered, "A friend." *So maybe,* he thought, *she has managed to get even another boom.*

About a month after his glimpse of that distant final bar of land across the waters at Suez, he was on the other side, battering through a late afternoon toward the northern Canal town of Kantara in a jeep driven by a pale bespectacled Israeli lieutenant. The two of them were passing now through a singed landscape which offered no answer or intelligence for what he had seen at Suez, but seemed merely a reflection, two riddles senselessly mirroring each other: a sprawling plain of craters with tilting telephone poles dangling useless lines, an occasional rusted wad of scorched unrecognizable metal left from the 1967 war. It was as if they had entered a terrain where some enormous violation of nature had taken place—that look of land which has been reduced to a simplicity fit for the minimal business of slaughter. The sun was burning low and murky ahead of them, and in the distance he could see tanks, brute and implacable as buffalo barging in fuming wallows of dust on across the scrubby desert toward the horizon. There, beyond the long faint fringe of trees that traced the Canal, taperings of smoke hung drowsily in the sky like random trailings of gauze with, intermittently, another abrupt and soundless spume upward among them. With a pause now in the Egyptian bombardment, they plunged on through Kantara, past oranges spilled from doorless entrance-ways, until at last they reached the Canal.

He tumbled clumsily, in a bulky flak vest and clanking helmet, out of the jeep and down into a sunken fortification, sandbagged slopes of gray grassless dust through which soldiers moved from burrow to burrow with a stooped tense quickness as if venturing momentarily into the atmosphere of another planet. Making his way then down a steep passageway, he abruptly stumbled into a bunker, and the stare of a man sitting erectly on the edge of a cot with a child's crayon drawing of flowers and spaceships on notebook paper taped to the corrugated-tin sheathing behind him—an Israeli doctor, now rumpled and bleary in the wan light of a single bulb over him, obviously just wrenched out of sleep, with an expression still on his face of stricken helplessness from the sudden clatter of feet and helmets down the tunnel toward him. They exchanged, for the next several minutes, with a dim steady hum from an electric generator somewhere, only a few halting phrases—the doctor still blinking, drawing his hand over his face and through his thinning ruffled hair, as if he had not yet quite reassembled himself out of that dreadful blankness into which he had awakened.

But more, it was as if, deep in these bunkers, all talk finally faltered and failed against the profound silence of a phenomenon beyond any articulation. Because by now—after Egypt and now Israel—the American had begun to suspect that what was actually under way here was an immense blundering collision of two different ages, a blind and vicious grappling of two different dialectics of life and experience: indeed, two realities, each barely comprehensible to the other. Before he left, he looked for a moment through one of the periscopes that, because of snipers, give the Israelis along the Canal fortifications their only view of the other side: the small precise circle passed slowly along an unending intricate tableau of walls and roofs and shadowy windows overlooking empty avenues in a glistening light like a tarnish of gold, as if it were part of another world, voiceless and without movement, but in which an absolute lethality lurked, with the waters of the Canal moving past it with a steady continuous rippling, in some calm soundless dream.

I

The Conflict from Afar

IN THE FIRST PLACE, this somewhat provincial and dislodged American journalist—baffled in the sunny wreckage of Suez, finding himself bumbling in helmet and flak vest down blind tunnels into Israeli bunkers at Kantara—had been propelled into it all, actually, by an editor's vagrant whimsy over a vodka Martini in a Thirty-second Street Manhattan restaurant one afternoon a full six months before. Reared in the remote broom-sage outback of the South, the son of a Baptist preacher, he had only infrequently ventured farther north than Virginia, much less beyond his own country and the comfortable familiar neighborhood of its history. Indeed, though he would soon discover he was more profoundly and innocently and hopelessly American than he had ever imagined, he had always felt, covertly and a little uneasily, that his true country was really the South. He was aware, in offices or at dinner parties in New York or New Haven or San Francisco, always of a subtle sensation of gawkiness and displacement, and usually wound up reverting to his plain aboriginal Southernness—in particular, its elementary gator-hide dialect. But in those years of his father's nomadic

3

pastorates through a succession of dusty little towns in Georgia and South Carolina, he had contracted somewhere a lingering half-manic furtive obsession to leave some scribbling of himself on the walls of his time before he vanished again: a desperate private skirmishing against oblivion. It had occurred to him now and then that it was quite possible he would merely wind up as a writer in that limbo of success between mediocrity and glory, able to sense the nature of great work but lacking some final component—audacity, sublime vanity, endurance, the capacity and willingness to go mad, whatever—to ever reach it. Anyway, he found himself at this point a journalist, a jackdaw of history: abruptly arrived at a faintly paunchy thirty, in appearance dissolute Appalachian, with only a shadow of the old ravenous gauntness of his youth still left in his face, but still secretly and irredeemably a kind of shabby romantic, still incorrigibly given to posturing. Some thirteen years had passed since, after reading *For Whom the Bell Tolls* and a short note in *Time* about a swashbuckling pack of guerrillas in Cuba's Sierra Maestra Mountains, he had stayed out of high school for a year, made three abortive Trailways bus trips to Miami trying to deliver himself into the Sierra Maestras, and managed the last time at least to get as far as Havana—which in Batista's day seemed a not altogether cheerless place for a seventeen-year-old to reconcile himself to failure in a larger adventure. But he had begun to be haunted that his epitaph might well be: "His was a life of brave beginnings. . . ." He had begun to wonder if, as a journalist, he had not become simply a collector of other people's experiences. He had, indeed, long been spooked by a remark of Faulkner's about the "immitigable chasm between all life and all print . . . those who can, do, and those who cannot and suffer enough because they can't, write about it."

THE CONFLICT FROM AFAR

One evening in the Arab quarter of Jerusalem, during dinner with a party of other journalists in an old colonial hotel—a magnificent stone-block anachronism with walkways under arbors through brimming technicolor gardens and antique wasp-waisted telephones that would all give a slight ting whenever a room was called, the dining room itself like a monastery chamber with a stone-slab floor under a low vaulted ceiling—a Jewish girl from Morocco suddenly leaned forward and inquired over the candlelight, in a tinkling voice that seemed to issue from a music box, "So you will spend a few weeks here, and then you will return to America and make large wise pronouncements about what is happening to all of us in this land, the Arabs and the Jews. But really, how can you know? How can you expect to know their suffering and despair that easily, without ever having experienced it even just a little bit yourself?"

Truthfully he had felt more than once a fleeting dreariness that journalism was merely some great amoral omniverous goat of the public's curiosity, journalists themselves a tribe of profane eunuchs, voyeurs who toured the tribulations and exultations and ragings over the earth, becoming eventually as stale and querulous as middle-aged spinsters. At such moments, it was his dim suspicion—perhaps even superstition—that there was no way actually to make a true deep passage through the fierce experience of another people, another place, without being seriously touched yourself, possibly even damaged: real understanding probably had to be personally expensive in some important way, had to issue finally out of one's own involvement and trauma. In fact, he fancied it would be like consciously entering into and committing oneself to some sort of debauchery or rapture in order that one might later withdraw from it and tell what it was like—a notion that vaguely invoked the image of Ulysses

5

lashing himself to the masthead so he could hear the sirens and survive to describe the experience—with always the implication, the danger, that one could claim by such an involvement and never be able to return to his innocence again. All this was probably why, back in the States after that leisurely proposal over Martinis at a sedate lunch, he had subsequently passed through the static winter months suspended in a profound inertia—a reluctance to depart that was most reminiscent of that luxurious lassitude which would settle over him when, engaged in a kind of play-ritual called Making Leaps during the summer mornings of his boyhood, he would crouch for long minutes on a tree limb from which he was to jump to another limb yards away, contemplating with a strange breathless deliciousness the intervening emptiness of mere air and light in which for an instant he would be spread weightless and helpless beyond recall, a brief void across which he could only be carried by the certainty, the momentum he mustered at that instant before the lunge. Actually, it was a compulsion—Making Leaps—that had continued on through his life, in one way or another. But for this one he had been poised now for almost five months, perhaps because he was not sure how much in front of him, after he let go, would be illusion, menace in shadows. So endlessly through those winter months he engaged in artificial departures, anticipations, and gropings, small tentative releases and extensions in his imagination while sitting in drawing rooms and lecture chambers still in the States. It was as if he were laboring to accomplish it without actually having to leave.

One mild spring evening, he sat in a Manhattan apartment with a small gathering of Jews, all of them editors and writers who had been to Israel, talking late into the night, and discovered that it had all suddenly become eminently lucid and manageable in the lamplight of this West Side apartment. Their speculations that evening were surrounded by walls of books—more books, it seemed, than his eye had ever encompassed in one glance in his life outside an actual public tax-supported library: covers of dull autumnal greens and browns and reds, between which, it appeared, all the furies and agonies and confusions loose elsewhere in the universe were contained. The effect of those numberless volumes around them, in fact, was one of insulation from accident, gently dispelling any sense of the imponderable, the daemonic at work in life. As they talked of what lay ahead of him, it was somehow like poring over a blueprint of a situation they already had in their possession—whatever might be missing was only a few steps away in those shelves. It was, on the whole, a reassuring evening.

Even more, he felt some particular quiet and unspoken snugness with these people—that sense of a curious secret intimacy which not only he but other Southerners he knew tend always to feel with Jews. He had an idea it had something to do with the fact that a lot of Southern boys are raised in homes presided over by mothers like Calvinist Sophie Portnoys, with the same passionate and relentless scrutinies, and with the same kind of plaintive beleaguered men attached to them. Also, in his case, he had been raised in a sedulous religiousness, isolated among an excruciatingly abstemious and conscious-stricken folk. In their passage through this world to a better land—the only land that counts—they had always seemed to him vaguely like displaced persons. The first memory he had of music was on a black winter night in the front parlor of their home in some little South Carolina junction: his father and mother were sitting with a few members of the congregation, and they were all listening to a phonograph playing, in a slow and deeply chambered bass bari-

7

tone, "Lead me gently home, Father . . . Lest I fall along the wayside, lead me gently home." Looking up at all of them gathered there in that front parlor, it had struck him, with some surprise and uneasiness, that behind their pleasant and comfortable composures they were all strangely discontent; who they were, how they were passing their lives, it was all not enough for them; they had a covert longing for some other place and some other existence waiting beyond them.

At the same time, the land of these people gathered now in this West Side apartment—Canaan—had, in a sense, been the second unseen landscape of his own childhood: he had grown up in the company of the patriarchs and prophets—Joshua on the mountains overlooking Jericho, King Ahab turning a corner in his vineyard to be confronted by the wrathful glower of old thorny Elijah, the dark brooding figure of Saul, Nathan, Jeremiah, Isaiah, Hosea. The Old Testament—with those almost Norse-like sagas of righteousness and wantonness, blood and absolution, all its clashings and smoke and magic—was probably the theatre from which he derived the dramaturgy of his own writing, so that he would, in fact, be venturing back into that land from which, through certain filtrations, he had always been working. If anything, it had all become amplified, relayed through the acoustics of the Southern Baptist sensibility: summer-night revival meetings reeling with contrition and exultation in whose fevers Judgment Day became an immediate and almost tangible reality, those old swooping hymns tolling with a grand deliberation in hot nights in the dim tragic glare of shadeless light bulbs—"There is a fountain filled with blood drawn from Immanuel's veins; and sinners, plunged beneath that flood, lose all their guilty stains. . . . Tomorrow's sun may never rise to bless thy long-deluded sight—Be saved, O tonight. . . ."—

while terrific and elemental conversions transpired along the altar. There was something about those services, the great knee-buckling undertow of those hymns, that left him with a special Gothic understanding forever after of the nature of doom: "Almost persuaded, Christ to receive . . . Angels are ling'ring near. . . . Seems now some soul to say, 'Go, Spirit, go Thy way, some more convenient day.' . . . Sad, sad, that bitter wail—'Almost—but lost!' " What was finally at work those nights was the immemorial struggle with the enchantments of this world. And these dynamics of guilt and redemption inevitably became a part of his vision of life; he had never been able to translate himself altogether beyond that heaving bulb-lit sentimentality.

So they shared, those in this West Side living room, a common experience and mythology in some wry and circuitous way. As much as for them, it was impossible for him to regard Israel as anything other than the second Exodus, not to mention probably the single most romantic event of modern history: a monument at last to the bareheaded efficacy of the poetic vision and spirit—beyond measuring are the obeisances owed Israel by all the harried romantics of the world. But finally, of course, it is an enigma, a phenomenon unaccountable except, incredibly, as a mystic event, a religious happening. ("Do you realize," someone had shouted several nights before over the bawl of voices in a narrow late-night tavern uptown, "this is the most absurd real-estate claim in the whole span of history!") But now as they talked, all slightly flushed, about this mystery accomplished six thousand miles away from them, he abruptly blurted that if he were Jewish, he would move to Israel instantly. There was a pause. He became aware of a momentary disconcertion in the room, and sensed then some final detachment from it all even here. At last, the handsome sensible woman sitting across from him mentioned with a faint distress that her daughter had already decided to emigrate to Israel. But, still awash in effusions, he asked what uneasiness kept them all from settling there. After a moment, another woman replied, "You want to know the truth? I think history has simply left the Jews with some deep skepticism, some automatic aversion, to really and irrevocably committing themselves to anything. Now, my daughter came back from a summer in Israel and told me, 'Mother, you just don't realize what's *happening* over there. It's a *serious* place. They are doing serious things, and they're all in it together.' All right. For the younger ones, maybe there's no problem. But for those who grew up before 1948, while they go to every bond rally and cheer the speeches and weep during the songs and give deeply of their money, still they don't really trust that this thing is for sure, for real. They just can't accept it. The Jews might be the most religious people to be found anywhere in the world, but deep down, I'll tell you, they don't even quite believe in God—*maybe,* you know, but who can say for sure?" But a girl slumped low on a couch, regarding the amber glints in her glass of Scotch with those expansive shelves of books banked imposingly around her, replied: "In the end, I suppose, that question is really unanswerable. . . ."

Also, not long before he left, he had attended a meeting in a suburban Atlanta library of an Arab friendship society—which, as it turned out, was composed principally of Arabs who form an unobtrusive but substantial colony in Atlanta's complex of universities. As with Israel, it was impossible for him to regard the Arabs now outside of those scenarios in the Sunday School rooms of his childhood. In that sooty and bulky brick citadel of a church set in a moldering downtown neighborhood of once-genteel gingerbread houses and oil-storage tanks and ice plants, with bare rooms of sallow tan and mint-green plaster-board which always seemed touched with a dull chill on wet winter mornings—tinged with an ancient sniff of dust, flies bumping against its dim windows and a small gas floor heater uttering a rim of brimming flame across the lip of its grille with a soft fluttering constancy—he had been left with an understanding of the Arabs that involved dark and sullen Ishmael, Abraham's makeshift half heir by his handmaiden Hagar, dispossessed by the miraculous last-minute arrival of Isaac and left to wander, brooding and uncomprehending, with his mother in the desert; or Esau, burly and wooly and undone by his own appetites, outwitted with a mere bowl of gruel by the pale wily pampered Jacob; or perhaps even Cain, rebuffed with his honest offering of toiled crops in favor of Abel's lamb. In some way, he assumed, it had all descended from those primeval aggrievements. But this Sunday afternoon in the linoleumed pastel-tinted conference hall of an Atlanta neighborhood library, they seemed an assembly of quiet and gentle folk, somewhat formal and subdued and exchanging ceremonious pleasantries, many of the men studiously communing with heavy meerschaum pipes. The speaker for this rather mild-mannered occasion was a former director of the United Nations Relief Agency in the Middle East, a large aging man with white hair and pale rheumy eyes, wearing a somewhat rumpled black suit, who devoted his waning energies now to an Arab-interests organization in Washington: "A distinguished national and, I might say, international figure," announced the moderator, "who I regret has not had the publicity that he deserves—but, of course, it seems that the space in the newspapers goes, shall we say, to other groups—" The moderator, a small and somewhat baggy man with dark dewy eyes, delivered this poignant aside with a decorous air of exquisite melancholy in the face of yet another affront: indeed, with the same vague self-abashment with which Nasser, in a television interview some weeks later, had seemed to smile in sheepish and half-apologetic embarrassment whenever he came to the slightest suggestion of any unmannerly, not to mention perhaps hostile, not to mention even violent, possibilities in their relationship with Israel. With this introduction, their man from Washington took the lectern and, after receiving from them a dutiful standing ovation, he confirmed for them that "Zionists have their influence everywhere it counts—in Hollywood, the networks. They tell their story, and they tell it well. But the thing that's overlooked is a tragedy has taken place: *another* people have been left without a country. . . . There are three million Palestinian refugees—outside the cease-fire lines, under occupation, or as restricted citizens in Israel. . . ."

As he proceeded, in a drowsing metronomic monotone, to recount for them, with statistical recitals, the evolution of the whole implacable impasse, they listened with meticulous attentiveness that was in itself one testament to their fortitude and endurance. "War itself can bring an end to the conflict," he eventually mused, "a war that could end in two ways: a holocaust in which both sides are left destroyed, or a war that Israel loses. I don't believe that any war Israel wins will bring peace. I don't think Israel can ever win a peace as she wants it, not in six, seven, a dozen wars. She'll only increase the unity and bitterness of the Arab countries. . . ." But in the end it seemed a curiously dispiriting message he delivered: "The Israelis are fighting for their very existence," he notified the gathering, "and they're more technically advanced, of course—more militarily advanced. . . ."

When the meeting was finished, a youth approached the visiting journalist and, gazing at him with the eyes of a mortally wounded deer, proceeded to explain that "most people have the wrong idea about Hitler, you see—" his voice soft and diaphanous in this assertion. "They think he was anti-Semitic, but he didn't hate the Jews at all. He simply recognized they were getting control of everything in Germany, and he wanted to keep Germany in the hands of the Germans. Hitler really wasn't like many people think of him; he was merely a German patriot. . . ." Later that evening, the American drove to the home of the meeting's moderator where they were all celebrating the speaker's visitation among them with a supper. It was one of those lush blue spring twilights in Atlanta that hang ambrosial with gardenias and wisteria. He found the moderator's house around a corner from a K-Mart shopping plaza, in a comfortable neighborhood of sleek lawns flecked with froths of dogwood and azaleas under high hushed pines. They were all gathered in a spacious downstairs den, along a massive sumptuously laden table—a cameo panorama of the whole Arab world: sober Lebanese businessmen, a dour bespectacled Palestinian with a moist handshake who introduced himself somberly by his "underground name," a silent Syrian with the fierce profile of a scimitar, and the speaker from Washington among them all, somewhat muzzy now but still maintaining a demeanor of casual eminence in their midst. They invited the journalist to take a plate and help himself from the table, but he somewhat awkwardly abstained, remained sitting off to one side merely sipping now and then from a Scotch-and-soda the flavor of extract of toothpick. Presently, they began passing down the table a worn yellowed volume published in the early nineteen-hundreds, written by some pundit philosopher of the time with a name like Hubbel or Hubbard, with passages, which they would pause

13

to read aloud, describing the Jews as descendants of a tribe of slaves and squatters who had never suffered from any sense of other people's property ever since they had revolted against their masters some four thousand years ago and been led, by a runaway slave, who himself had murdered one of his masters, on a trek of thieving and spoilage. They all listened to these readings with small wistful smiles and shakings of the head. One of them turned to the journalist finally and declared, "You know, it is very difficult to be an Arab in this country. Even though most of these you see around you tonight are citizens of this country, yet we are Arabs. You have no idea what it is like to be an Arab living in the United States. No one around us truly understands the situation. I must tell you, it is a very lonely feeling. . . ."

Since 1967, the Egyptians have maintained their diplomatic mission in Washington at the rear of the Indian Embassy, and going there one afternoon to clear his visa, the American had the impression, as soon as he had shut the door, that a scurrying of voices had abruptly ceased everywhere around him—he glimpsed a face peering at him from a stairway leading down to the basement, quickly vanishing to be replaced a moment later by another face. Then, after a wait of several minutes in an anteroom, he was taken into the office of Dr. Ghorbal—a diminutive man with an immaculate precise manner in which, as they sat talking about the American perspectives on the Middle East, there was only the faintest tinge of a fine melancholy. But then an ancient and white-jacketed Ethiopian entered the room, stooped and grizzled and the color of sodden ashes, bearing a silver tea service, and with a sudden flurry of barking from Ghorbal, he arranged the saucers and chinaware with sluggish fingers, answering Ghorbal with a short guttering of consonants —this momentary communication between them some stray murmur from another universe.

And at last, in a condition of deep bleariness one late evening, after a disheveled last hour of phone calls and travel-check negotiations and lurching cabs, he flew out of New York—the plane immediately absorbed into a fog in which all motion and direction and even time seemed to have vanished. There was no sense of separation from his own familiar continent; its edge passed away beneath him at some point unseen, unaware, unremarked.

He awoke to find that sunshine had infiltrated the cabin. Then, still with nothing below him but a dull measureless blue haze, there began a slight and lasting sensation of buoyancy, and presently the earth began dimly reassembling far beneath him: mountains, wrinkled and brown as the skin of dried apples, the faintest shining capillary traces of rivers—an appearance of innocent familiarity that actually disguised an alien continent which had been slipped under him in the night as he slept. Approaching Rome now, the plane passed low over an earth which actually held, beneath a trivial flotsam of telephone wires and filling stations from this latest century's tide, an ancient pagan knowledge: the memory of a time of bronze and blood and torch smoke and incomprehensible hysterias and exultations presided over by forgotten gods, thinly populated by those scraggly runtish forebears of the race before vitamin pills and pasteurization and psychiatry whose puny furies and lustings have come to us inflated into the epic and heroic. That morning in Rome, he saw the Colosseum, with those remains in its pit of a carefully constructed village, the artificial streets and shelters through which lions swirled after human beings under the public's gaze in the stands, bespeaking now a casual cruelty that seems unimaginable, insane, belonging to a remote world sunk deep into the past whose only intimations come to us now, as Alberto Moravia says of *Fellini Satyricon,* "as the memory of a dream . . . whose meaning has been lost . . . obscure, half-obliterated, absurd, mysterious."

During the hours of his layover in Rome's glassy clangoring airport, he became gradually aware that, very near to Cairo now, he had already entered different crosscurrents. Also waiting at the gate for his flight were two Chinese Communists—the superenemy glimpsed!—who had ventured from that far galaxy where it was contended the next new species of man had emerged which would in patient time inherit the earth. With furtive but ferocious curiosity, then, were these two specimens eyed by the doomed Westerners around them. Dressed in identical plain blue prim uniforms that suggested a sewing-machine factory, maintaining the ascetic otherworldly gravity of a pair of Jehovah's Witnesses or Salvation Army regulars, they stood carefully off to themselves, somewhat close together, both of them with their arms tightly crossed, their lips occasionally pursing at the same time and foreheads faintly puckering as if on common secret signal with simultaneous thoughts. For the most part, they were totally impervious to the peerings around them —except for one moment, when the shorter of the two calmly withdrew a handkerchief from his front trouser pocket and quickly, discreetly, wiped both his palms dry. An hour later, in the plane on the way to Cairo, the short one abruptly rose from his seat and strolled up to the magazine rack at the front of the cabin. After some sober rummaging, he finally withdrew a copy of *Holiday* magazine and was walking back to his seat when, for some reason, he suddenly paused, then went back up the aisle, replaced the magazine in the rack, and returned, empty-handed, to his seat beside his companion.

The plane hammered on now against the late afternoon, with Egypt—Africa—finally drawing near at the end of this sustained lunge backward against the spin of the earth. He felt now an odd dizziness like that always brought to him by those old uncertainly blinking newsreels from the turn of the century showing the soundless blaring of leaders, the passionate jittery surgings and marchings of multitudes, all now long dead. This same sensation of dislocation he had also always experienced whenever he visited places where his forebears had dwelt, contemplating the countrysides and houses that had contained, long before he was born, their daily existences, their presences, their lost voices.

But this was a voyage not only back beyond his own existence, but back into the primordial mystery of a society that had existed before his own hemisphere had even been dreamed of.

Where It Began

> Then Pharaoh called also the wise men and the sor-
> cerers, now the magicians of Egypt. . . . And the Lord
> hardened the heart of Pharaoh, king of Egypt, and he
> pursued after the children of Israel, all the horses and
> chariots of Pharaoh, and his horsemen, and his army,
> and overtook them encamping by the sea. . . . And
> Moses stretched forth his hand over the sea. . . . And
> the waters returned, and covered the chariots, and the
> horsemen, and all the host of Pharaoh. . . .
> —The Book of Exodus

LYING IN A BREATHLESS HEAT far up the Nile in the interior of Egypt, the ancient Pharaonic city of Luxor is now more
or less a colonial ghost town, with shaded carriages still clopping
along its river-front boulevard in the muffled late afternoon
transporting sun-pinked camera-slung tourists with plastic souvenir bags instead of braided British commissioners with their
cologned ladies on their way to tea.

He had flown up that morning from Cairo—and now, from
a dock below the balconies of the Winter Palace Hotel, he set
out for the far riverbank in a narrow-awninged ferry launch
with a clattering gas motor like a tractor engine, chugging
creakily and patiently on across the sprawling, glazed surface
of the Nile back into the furthest sunstruck silences of antiquity.
On the other bank, a waiting car carried him through a waste-

18

land like a photograph negative, blinding white bluffs against a dark blue sky almost near blackness, all of it blank of any sound or movement, life, any trace of the passage of centuries, civilizations, mortal events. Finally they reached the Valley of the Kings, the car stopping before what seemed a scattering of holes, dark mouths gaping mute and meaningless in the sun. But venturing down their dim chill gullets—down passageways illuminated by light bulbs in rock leading to broken sarcophaguses— he discovered a long profusion of colors and shapes like violent luxurious poled perfumes of that past sucked and held abeyant from the total obliteration accomplished aboveground: an interminable tattooing over those stone walls, unfathomable chronicle of crownings, processions, with hawk-head deities, sedate warfares, calm multiple beheadings, all done with an odd crude simplicity under clumsily starred skies like the laborious drawings of a fourth-grader. It seemed to whisper some civilization of precocious terrible children filling these last corridors to extinguishment with hectic myriad comic-strip panels of all their small familiar tranquillities and beguilements and assertions, a rampant obsessive cartooning suffusing the walls and corners and even ceilings like some pell-mell graffiti, as if this were actually the aboriginal artistic impulse, the common genesis of both *Paradise Lost* and the epigrams on the walls of fillingstation rest rooms.

Then, as the car carried him back toward the ferry, he saw their enormous constructions looming almost incidentally above the alluvial ink-green fields along the Nile, most of them left massively askew by the jostlings of subsequent earthquakes and armies. In the temples near Luxor, he found walls and columns scribbled with the graffiti of successive tides of invasion and pilgrimage—"Holroyd 1837 . . . Rimbaud," crude notchings in ancient Latin, Greek, that had the same hasty awkwardness of those anonymous initials one sees littered across rock cliffs along mountain highways in North Carolina; it was as if they had paused here to leave these labored cramped etchings ignorant that history would even remember their passage and plunder, mindless that two thousand years later they would be known with awe as the Romans, the Greeks. But what stunned him in this mighty rubble of pillars and effigies—abiding now in a titanic tongueless oblivion of chittering sparrows—was the epic desperation of those vanished slight four-foot-eight men to magnify themselves, to duplicate themselves in colossal redundancy with colonnades of identical monoliths: man beginning on earth instantly in vanity and bombast, with his history seeming ever since more or less a procession of the same.

The inhabitants of Luxor now seem to live in a kind of affectionate gossipy intimacy with these kings of Egypt's dawn— a fondness, one senses, arising out of an assurance that these ancestral giants had looked out for them by supplying these ruins to provide their progeny forever after with a livelihood in tips. In remote corners of roofless temples, under slumped pillars and behind mammoth pedestals, the American glimpsed meager tidy pallets where many of them sleep at night. His own guide, the latest member of a professional dynasty going back to his great-great-grandfather, was himself now sixty-eight, with a face like mahogany-colored leather, and a bit winded after each steep climb out of the tombs into the blast of the sun, but facing eight more years before his ordained retirement. When they first set out in the ferry launch, he had produced from somewhere in the engulfing folds of his snowy robe a neatly printed business card: "Gasem Ahmed, Guide. Speaks English, French, German & Italian. 48 Years Experience. Luxor, U.A.R."

He was, he solemnly reported, "a pure Moslem. All my years, never take one drink of alcohol, not even beer pass my lips. My wife I bouth in Alexandria for five hundred pounds, dot is one wonderful woman—I tell her, she deh first and deh last, but she don believe me, I donno why." Before very long, he announced, "I like very much someday to see deh Fifth Avenue in New York City. I been in dot *Life* magazine and I been in dot *Look* magazine, when deh come here both once. Maybe your magazine could fix it so I come over. Dot Nasser, he awfully hard, he don give you a thing. He don let anybody out now because of the Israelis, but if your magazine write to him a letter, I think Nasser wouldn't say anything. Maybe so? *Merci beaucoup.* Dot Fifth Avenue one place Ahmed like to walk and see." As they were proceeding to the tombs, he kept speculating in his soft and lilting singsong, "Maybe I'm descendant of dese Pharaohs, I don know. Everybody say I look like Ramses II," and whenever, deep in the crypts, they would come on the dim sepia figure of some Pharaoh, Ahmed would strike a profile pose by match glow close against it: "Me. See?—me." Trudging on through the temples languidly, flourishing his fly-whisk, his battered Florsheim shoes making small mutters in the dust, he mused in a low melancholy murmur, "But deh Pharaohs, deh become decadents. Over dere, now, the tomb of Queen Hatshepsut—we don like her because she was very bawdy queen. She not my friend, I'm afraid," and he paused now and then, after reporting some casual royal atrocity, to shake his head in awed disapproval and sigh, "Ahh, deh were very intelligent, most intelligent, but very cruel. Very cruel—tsk-tsk-tsk . . ." Accompanying them was a pale and earnest young man with sandy muttonchop whiskers from New York, an Egyptologist whose avid and elaborate passion for the subject was somewhat complicated by the fact he suffered from an aversion to sun and heat, and whenever the two Americans began to flag, Ahmed would croon happily, "*Coo*-rage. *Coo*-rage," a delicate and elegant summons with which no doubt he had been gently tugging faltering cultural pilgrims along for forty-eight years. "Look now dese acrobatics. Look dese warrd-iors. Look dot fish, how real. . . ." He paused once before a whimsically pornographic tableau, and, with a quick flip of his fly-whisk, reported in a faintly scandalized mumble, "I seen many German ladies make deah hosbands wait for dem while day climb up deah and measure deh penises. Yes."

Lying still along the Nile are the moist low fields and huddled settlements which have lingered on for the five thousand years since these temples and monoliths—a dense and precariously fertile infestation, as myriad and endless as the pageantry arrayed over the walls of the tombs, of donkeys, threshers, buffalo, water carriers, reapers all absorbed placidly in their innumerable simultaneous labors like one of Breughel's paintings of a medieval harvest. Across the face of this land move slow mute figures of women wrapped in raven-black cloth, passing simple warrens of mud-brick huts pinched and patted out of the very dirt under date palms, with pajamaed children flurrying in puffs of dust among the bald lanes through shatters of chickens. The only signs of any progression of history are the trivial adornments of telephone poles, a powder-blue building on the Nile like a frumpish Crimean palace which houses the local chapter of the Arab Socialist Party, and—clamoring everywhere from alleyways, even pulsing faintly across the quiet remains of the temples—the sound of radios, insistent and inexhaustible, that essential element, the oxygen (all the Middle East, in fact, seeming if not the original at least the ultimate Radioland) of the current government which presumes it is presiding over this ageless primeval society: the revolutionary khakied radio republic some four hundred miles down the river at Cairo.

Landing in a late afternoon five days before at the Cairo airport, it seemed he had been dropped into a languorous dream of intelligible echoing voices, officials in discreetly soiled white uniforms who exchanged his money for an inscrutable oversized currency tinted in Easter pastels. Clapped by multitudinous hands into a cab, he rode through terrain of taffy-colored sand scribbled with barbed wire, past wooden sentry towers and the bland walls of military installations, and then a spacious suburb of walled snuff-yellow stucco villas with flowers a lipstick red, reaching at last the edge of Cairo. He found himself now entering a city like some living many-layered Troy—some old massive millstone still thick with the residue, the intermingled pulps and chaff of all its slow immense turnings and gristings through the four thousand years since Luxor and Thebes: Alexander, the Caesars, the Turks and Mamelukes, Napoleon, the Europeans. In the seethe of its streets, humankind dwelt still in its primordial condition, as close to the dust as lizards and living the existence of lizards: women with burnt-out faces hunkering at alleyways from which issued a breath like that of monkey cages, with small children standing and nursing from both bared breasts; fellahin in their liquid flimsy nightshirts trudging along railroad tracks in some continuous procession out of nothingness into nothingness through a timeless arrested sundown; others sitting in small yellow dirt parks carefully sipping from filter-tip cigarettes with their knees spread under their gowns, wearing rubber shower sandals with ribbed nylon socks rolled down around bony powdered ankles (in the mornings right after dawn, he would see them squatting up and down the slopes of the Nile, one hand clutching a rock above them for balance, to defecate). A motorbike passed them with a sidecar in which a man was grasping the shirt front of a small boy, his head bobbling and dangling with the bumps, who could have been either drowsing or only an hour or so dead. Down an interminable succession of dirt side streets, the American glimpsed milling tunnels of trade in hot tea, cabbages, tin pots, tallow-white chicken carcasses, aphrodisiacs, incidental newsstand pornography, illustrated pamphlets of Leda and the Swan. (There lurks in the city, he was to discover, a kind of musing miasmal sexuality, in some profound way defeated but still obsessive. Walking down his hotel corridor, he once passed two men standing just inside an open door, clutching each other and weeping hopelessly, and as he was fitting his key into his lock he glanced back to see one of them walking on down toward the elevators with the other leaning into the hall calling after the departing figure with violent shouting sobs.) The voices in the streets were all yelping in a language that sounded like a desperate bubbling of mellow vowels from the constricted gutturals of a progressive strangulation—an uproar through which streetcars clanged savagely with a dry snapping of sparks beneath billboard advertisements done in florid and vicious art reminiscent of those brazen unholy depictions on the signs outside carnival sideshow tents. Taxicabs in a numberless rampancy kept up a constant babble of puny horn bleats. In all this, an occasional funeral procession, black figures walking behind a black coach pulled by horses, coiled briefly into sight and then vanished into the crowds again.

"One can only thank God they are Moslem," a foreign professor speculated at dinner several evenings later, "that they don't take alcohol and there is imposed on them that Victorian decorum of their religion. If these Moslem disciplines and abstinences were removed, they would be uncontrollable, it would be unimaginable." On another evening—in an alley café with a roof of cane thatching against the stars, birds twittering in suspended cages—an Egyptian government official told him, "The truth is the Egyptian simply cannot live without religion. Whether Re, Amon, Zeus, Dionysius, Christ, or Allah, they have had to have a religion—some religion—for all their four thousand years." The American seemed at times to catch this desperation in the sunset cries of the muezzin—lingering brokenhearted howls of longing after God, full of an old and inconsolable woe. Then, one afternoon, he was taken to a Coptic cathedral in Cairo by an Egyptian student whose sister and brother-in-law had been among the Arabs he had met that afternoon back in Atlanta. The student had wanted to be a priest, and even though he was studying now, under the instructions of his father, to be an electrical engineer, he had remained unwifed, celibate—a youth captured by an overwhelming shyness against which he was always struggling. He was dressed this afternoon in a solemn black suit with white shirt and thin black tie, holding his hands gently cupped at his middle coat button as if to receive the communion water as they ascended the cathedral steps. Constructed to ornament a portion of Saint Mark's remains recently sent to Cairo by the Vatican, the edifice seemed a ludicrous extravagance, looming out of the weltering scrabble of misery all around it, in a state of indefinite incompletion, all work stopped because of the war and no date set for its resumption: dirt aisles and naked brick walls crudely mortared and webbed with strings, light bulbs dangling from long cords, and scaffolding reaching up into high vaulted spaces where the few voices around them died in small lost echoes. The student led him on around to the rear—a short walk past mimosa trees where two earth-drab beggars were squatting along an ageless earth-drab wall over a small brilliant fire in the afternoon heat—to the small rotunda shrine in whose center was set a chest-high marble sarcophagus containing the unseen cherished fragments of Saint Mark. For several minutes, he gazed at the rainbow-hued murals around the wall, illustrations of Saint Mark's life, and then turned to discover that the student had been standing for several moments now at the sarcophagus, his slight fragile hands lying lightly atop the marble while his lips were stirring faintly in some secret inaudible utterance, perhaps in yet another struggling explanation of his broken promise, his exile now in the secular world. And in that instant, he realized in this wispy abashed student the phenomenon of a belief outside history, larger than such meager details as dubious bones, larger than all the incidental refuse of mortal earthly existence from which all science and cynicism and frivolousness derive: a belief more complete and absolute and inviolate than anything known in the West since the medieval period of grace, indeed, a faith finally incomprehensible, which was its own reality, created its own realities, so that suddenly the American actually *was* in the presence of the remnants of Saint Mark; he had come into brief intersection with a single thin tenuous line of physicality from the dark maelstrom of the past all the way to a taste of wine in lantern light among low voices and the fleeting touch of a gaunt figure in an upper room in Judea.

In fact, he began to have the sense, after a few days in Cairo, that he was in the midst of some cataclysmic implosion of time. Coinciding with this primal religiousness and the primeval moil of mankind in the streets was a disheveled exertion—cement trucks, electric generators, power lines, all the rump-side ganglia of progress—to conjure forth a brave new technological society. Hotel phones, lifted from cradles shaped like crocodile paws, offered erratic approximations of communication; closet doors opened to the blinking of uncertain tube lights from Rumania; lamps murmured with transparent low-wattage bulbs. With this exertion now additionally harassed by Israel, Cairo had a curious look of World War II: there were desultory blackouts after sundown, traffic proceeding with a nervous winking of dim headlights past official buildings whose windows were all daubed in blue paint. The ubiquitous military paraphernalia on the streets had an archaic pre-nuclear look, like that in old newsreels of the Allied occupations of Italian towns, back when war was still a motorized matter, with jeeps and trucks painted a dull butterscotch rumbling back and forth beneath billboards on which girls coiffed like Dorothy Lamour and Betty Grable lounged saucily with the vivid smiling lips and stout shoulders of the forties.

The fact is the government of Egypt is now engaged not only in a war with Israel but in a second interior war against Egypt's past. This second war is conducted from the newer spare geometric buildings of plaster and glass—soldiers clustered like wasps at their sandbagged entranceways, a slightly dingy and secondhand look about them after ten or twelve years—which contain the clerks and engineers and technocrats of a revolution. By the standards of surrounding history, this revolution is approaching middle age. Sitting in an office in one of these buildings one afternoon, the American was informed by a government subminister, "I will be very honest with you—there is no doubt that we are still struggling to bring this country into the twentieth century." Such a feat would seem more staggering and complicated to negotiate than the accomplishment of the Pyramids—a quantum leap across the inertia of accumulated centuries of stasis.

Indeed, almost immediately after disembarking from the plane at the airport, he had begun to suspect that the essential economy on which all of Egypt was secretly sustaining itself was the "baksheesh" industry. That soft whispered plea, the opening palms instantly began to nibble at his attention, following him through every turn, even through the cab window, like some siege of piranha fish, the unblinking beseeching stares regarding him calmly, at once unhoping and ravenous, out of a condition of human desolation that had at first stunned and bewildered him. For three years now, Egypt has been suffering through a tourist drought. An old guide at the Giza Pyramids outside Cairo told him, "Yes, I have many friends at the Miamia Beach, the New York City, and the Los Angeles also, I know these many people over years. But since 1967, with the Israeli planes, I have not seen them, they have stopped coming any more, they are all gone." At the bottom of the road leading up to the Pyramids, there is usually gathered a large restless congregation of guides atop tasseled camels. Whenever a cab passes carrying anyone with a camera, they wheel and pursue it in a mad dusty stampede all the way up the hill like Indians after a stagecoach, milling around the passenger when he gets out, with a desperate amiability that threatens to trample him. At the Sphinx below the Pyramids, at the tombs at Luxor, they kept materializing out of dust and heat like dark wraiths, filtering after the American through the ruins with tawdry scraps of gaiety snatched at random over years from passing Americans: "What's up, doc? Everything copacetic? All A-O.K.? See you later, alligator!" After a while, their bold smiles in burnt bony faces began to seem like the grinning of cannibals. But here and there he found this assiduous forlorn enterprise had been touched with a curious revolutionary integrity: on a main Cairo boulevard he was stopped by a street boy of about fourteen who, rebuffed in his offer of a shoeshine, asked for a cigarette and then, after accepting it, announced, "Now you give me this, I shine your shoes free." He pursued the American doggedly through perilous intersections of traffic, vaulting over sidewalk railings with his shoe box, shouting, "But I must! I cannot let you give me cigarette for nothing. Is not *good* for me. You understand?"— walloping his chest—"Is not *right* for me in here, to take cigarette for nothing," until he was virtually sobbing, tears actually in his eyes. Perhaps in such small alterations, such nuances, are revolutions truly registered.

On another afternoon, at the end of a series of bare corridors patched with damp mortar and lit by feebly glowing mosquito filaments, he found Egypt's Undersecretary for Planning, a cordial plumpish buoyant man in shirt sleeves smoking L & M cigarettes. Sitting on the edge of his chair in an office through which there swirled a steady tumbleweed of papers, clerks, graphs, charts, with the telephone beside him regularly giving a thin rattle, he would pause now and then to slap some passing paper to his desk long enough to scribble notes and corrections on it, while he declared, "The official working day in Egypt comes to an end around two o'clock in the afternoon, but we here have been working on through the rest of the days now, on into the evenings sometimes. And it seems we are inching ahead. Agriculture, of course, is our chief economic factor, and we are now a net exporter, which is very good. Oil can go skyward. In the next five years"—he stopped to study a catalogue of more statistics laid before him by an assistant, an earnest man in a blue suit with beltless trousers, a thin snipped toothbrush mustache his one debonair flourish, his back slightly humped and his hands drawn in at his waist, one hand steadily scratching the top of the other—"we will be expanding to steel compounds to triple our production. In fact, the crisis since 1967 is one reason I believe we're faring so well. It's given everyone, you know, this feeling of necessity, of responsibility. . . ."

"I assure you," melodiously intoned the genial Minister of National Guidance, soon to depart for his new post as Ambassador to France, as he opened for his visitor a Byzantine-patterned cigarette box, "Durrell was writing about Egypt as it was forty years ago. Egypt is not like that today." But before long the American came across a kind of inner society of a quiet domestic community of refugees from the prerevolutionary years who gather now regularly in the lilac cool of the evenings at Cairo's Gezira Sporting Club. The club sits on an island in the Nile—a genteel vestige of England's custodial presence bowered under low trees among expansive greens, with a dim circular bar of parquet floors and walnut wainscoting along lemony walls. Through open doors sparrows flutter to snitch nuts from the bowls under the lamps, and then flutter back out again into the declining afternoon where Mercedes are glimmering leisurely past long porches of wicker chairs, and waiters float back and forth under the trees in luminous white robes, carrying trays of rum fizzes. One perfumed sundown, he found a few of these kindred souls sitting and talking among themselves on a patio, and while distant figures attired in white moved up and down a bowling lawn behind them, they spun gossamer nostalgias in the blue evening air about another time, gentle ironies about the present. Someone mentioned the United States ambassador: "He is a rather rough man, you know. No delicacy, a rather rough sense of humor, actually. . . ." They were, altogether, a com-

pany of eminently pleasant and congenial men. Among them
was a former Egyptian general who had been abruptly disposed
of by Nasser in 1956—a mild cheerful man of a clumsy bulk as
if he had been saved and hammered together out of haphazard
plank ends, a delicate proper mustache dabbed on his huge face:
with a painful earnestness, he began explaining Egypt's essential
peaceableness while he steadily fingered a necklace of Islamic
prayer beads until, in a kind of affectionate impatience, the man
beside him snatched the beads out of his hands, the general
proceeding to furl up the bottom of his tie into a tight little roll
as he continued to discourse. Presently, they were joined by a
younger man in dark glasses and a golfing sweater who vaguely
resembled a more heartily fed Woody Allen; he was introduced
as the son of Egypt's largest landowner before Nasser: "This
fellow here, now, it was his kind they had the revolution for.
Out there on his estate, he used to hunt *people*."

The American went on with them for supper in an apartment
belonging to an engineer now in his robust fifties whose father
had reputedly been making two million dollars a year before
Nasser and had been somewhat distressed by this playboy son
of his, Fawzi, who so far had proceeded through three marriages. His den rather evoked a room in a fraternity house on the
campus of a Midwestern state university; a giant mock-up bottle
of Johnnie Walker Black Label rested atop a stereo playing
Tom Jones, Richard Harris, the theme from *Midnight Cowboy*.
Before long, a few women arrived who were attached with vary-
ing degrees of formality to the men there, and it soon began to
emerge to this American journalist, even in Egyptian, that several arabesque games and arrangements were quietly pending
here, a continuous play of baroque prospects. He had already
detected an understanding between an Egyptian information

official—a somewhat sober and morose fellow, now a little dewy
with sweat, in heavy horn-rim glasses, with a dark smudge of
savagely shaven beard—and a towering strawy Dutch blonde
with a small bitten face, nearing the frayed years of forty but
still lithe and handsomely preserved, who was herself married
to a Mediterranean diplomat. During supper, she suddenly
looked at the American and announced, "You screwed us, you
know, in Indonesia," a proclamation which the Egyptian information official obviously understood to be a sexual flare, the
first sniff of a developing gamy coziness. He grew progressively
more taut, and when the American happened to mention that he
had been born in January, the official abruptly turned to him
and imparted the news, "You will probably get cancer. Yes,
that's right, I saw the statistics someplace, very responsible medical statistics; people born in January always die from cancer
more than people born in any other month." A few minutes
later, the official stood and remarked a little metallically he
would like to leave now. The woman merely fluttered her hand
from her chair and tinkled, "Goodbye. . . ." But he remained
standing, his eyeglasses glittering in the lamplight, until, at last,
the woman got up and left with him, leaving behind now only
the American and Fawzi and an Egyptian doctor. As soon as he
heard the elevator doors in the hall bump shut behind them,
Fawzi groaned, "Ahh, is she not a beauty? There has been this
thing with the two of them for at least the past seven years, yet
she stays married to that husband of hers, a very tall and handsome man himself who does not give a damn for her. But with
her and Akrouk, do you know, there is no sex? For the last five
years, absolutely"—he slapped his knee "—no sex! This I know.
She does not finally enjoy the act. Superb in everything right up
to the act itself. But Akrouk is absolutely dedicated to her. He

takes such treatment from her—ahhh, he takes such suffering. But if she were to point to you and say, 'Akrouk, kill him,' he would kill you right there, just like snapping the fingers." And then, with the night tapering into the vacant stillness of early morning in the steady bleary glow of the lamps, Fawzi and the doctor fell to lamenting, over the last watery Scotch in their glasses, the passing of the great courtesans: "Magnificent women, were they not? You remember them? Nothing whatsoever of whores about them, never did it have anything to do with the money, but for love, they were women who simply lived for love. Cultured, beautiful—my God! You would find them at all the best parties, with diplomats and government ministers, they were simply a part of great society. But they have all gone, haven't they? All of it is gone. You know, there just aren't any serious affairs any more. With the young people now, sleep with one, sleep with another, it doesn't matter—your girl leaves you, so what? You'll just find another one tomorrow somewhere. It's all merely functional now. Something has been lost in life, good friend. There was a time—ah, I remember it—you were in love with a woman, you would always be afraid you would lose her, she would always be afraid she would lose you. There would be scenes at parties. But you *gave* yourself then. Love was *important* then. . . ."

On the first Thursday of every month, a concert is given in Cairo by a sixty-two-year-old Egyptian diva named Oum Kalsoum, who has been for decades now a kind of torch singer, folk singer, soul singer to the entire Arab world, speaking to the most ancient heart of their Arabness like some combination of Edith Piaf, Mahalia Jackson, Judy Garland, and Sophie Tucker. She has become a phenomenon in the Middle East, and her monthly concerts, lasting from around tea until two in the morning, are seismic events for which private Caravelle and Lear jets come skidding into Cairo's airport for days ahead, bearing sheiks and sultans and Prime Ministers from Morocco to Kuwait. As was usual on the nights of her concerts, Cairo's informal underground of prerevolutionary émigrés, the American now among them, gathered this Thursday evening in May at the night club down a short alley from the cinema hall where she would perform, with a quiet brisk dispatch getting securely and comfortably drunk as soon as they arrived. Presently, a woman entered whose browned face was puckered in merriment, black eyes twinkling, like an elfin monkey under a lush mane of black hair raked straight back: she had a certain laved look of money about her, like a faint shimmer of coins along her limbs. Already a trifle awash, she was on the arm of a pretty perfumed fluorescent youth, also lushly maned, whom she introduced to Fawzi by his first name and sang, "Isn't he beautiful? . . . ." Fawzi later told the American she was an Egyptian named Lani, who had been carefully and thoroughly seasoned in European schools and was still a formidable business figure in Cairo. From Fawzi's other shoulder, she looked across at the American and said, "That may be, but I'm not nearly as rich as I once was. But then, none of us are, are we, Fawzi?" She turned to greet Akrouk, the information official, who seemed somewhat more chipper this evening and wedged himself onto a stool beside her at the bar, declaring, "You and I, Lani, when we are both of us past sex, when that is behind us, we will marry and spend our lives with nothing but beautiful flowers and music," and she reached forward, pulling his head toward her, and kissed his damp cheek and told him, "I adore you, Akrouk. I just adore you. That is an appointment."

Through the pent uproar of the voices around him, the American caught occasional dim wellings of applause from the concert hall, like a faint sibilance of surf from some far shore. The people around him seemed engaged in a kind of calculated ritualized berserkness, and he thought then of a passage from Styron: *"They slept restlessly, dreaming loveless dreams. . . . There was dance music and, later, Mozart, a song of measureless innocence that echoed among lost ruined temples of peace and brought to their dreams an impossible vision: of a love that outlasted time and dwelt even in the night, beyond the reach of death and all the immemorial, descending dusks . . . they stirred and turned. . . . They were painted with fire, like those fallen children who live and breathe and soundlessly scream, and whose souls blaze forever. . . ."* But his indulgence in this melodramatic fancy—one handhold, at least, a metaphor, while he sat at his bar, adrift and stranded, feeling rather like a pike fish lost in a school of gorgeous anemones—was gradually dispelled by the realization that there was something oddly dated about the scene: it was as if they had all only now belatedly arrived at a style of life that pertained forty years ago to Paris, belonging actually in *The Sun Also Rises.* Suddenly he heard Lani's voice: "What are you doing, why don't you relax? You sit there like you're trying to figure us all out or something. God *damn* you Americans—I do agree with Toynbee, you *are* the most dangerous people on the face of the earth." And he could only answer with a mute grin, while he thought but did not say, *Not just Americans. Anglo-Saxons, including even Toynbee. Any Anglo-Saxon plopped down here like a cold toad in all this—even Durrell, probably, which was why he could go off later and write about it. . . .*

After a while, he noticed a tall quiet man in his thirties

35

passing through, pausing only briefly at each huddle, saying
nothing, only listening for a moment and then moving on,
dressed in a sedate neat suit with a harshly barbered haircut
that gave him the look somehow of an F.B.I. agent. Fawzi
identified him as an Egyptian fighter pilot, one of the few who
had not only managed to survive for several years but had
actually downed a number of Israeli planes. Now a kind of
one-man R.A.F. for Egypt, he still flew regular missions, assuming each day once again the singular burden of having become
by some perverse accident one of his luckless nation's few
answers to the legendary skills of a whole fleet of enemy pilots,
in this unimaginable loneliness entering each day a dimension
of silence and blue space and death and desperate craft into
which none of his own people could follow him, a dimension
now from which he could never fully withdraw, and in which
the enemy pilots were actually more intimate company to him
than these people whom he seemed to regard now as through
some pane of glass, forever removed from their breath and
warmth and touch. And yet, as Fawzi reported, he kept returning to this night club, could be found here each evening around
ten o'clock: "But he refuses to talk. He won't even tell you what
he does, even when he knows that you know anyway. You ask
him, he says he is a playboy. Several times I have tried just to
engage him in a little polite conversation, you know, but he
doesn't want it. No. Nobody can make friends with him, it
seems. So I finally said, To hell with him, if that's the way he
wants it. O.K.—I don't worry about it any longer." A few minutes later, the American saw the pilot sitting alone on a bench
off by the door, his face absolutely expressionless, simply watching the others in the night club, all of whom had ceased to
notice him now. A moment later, he glanced back again, and
discovered the bench was empty, the pilot gone.

Then, with an intermission in the concert at the cinema hall, more people began entering the club, among them Nasser's daughter in a small party moving to a table, causing around them only briefly lifted eyebrows, suspended glasses, faint down-tugs at the corners of mouths. At last, sometime after midnight, he wandered with a group up the alleyway to the cinema hall where the concert had resumed, carrying their drinks in their hands while the faun who had arrived with Lani danced along a wall beside them. They formed a dense cluster at an open door in the rear of the auditorium, the dour young khakied guards casting furtive glowers at their flushed faces, their clothes, the glasses in their hands. On the stage, a kind of private salon orchestra, dressed in tuxedos, was already at work, with Oum Kalsoum sitting before them at the center of the footlights dressed in a simple green gown, absolutely motionless in her chair, her hands on her knees and a scarf in her lap: from that distance, she resembled a somewhat humorless and buxom great-aunt with dyed black hair drawn glassily back in a bun (Fawzi whispered, "She didn't marry until she was fifty-five—and then it was to a skin doctor") waiting while the orchestra continued what seemed after a while to be an inexhaustible overture, abject sawing moan's twining through each other, a stunningly wild din out of the desert, their common genesis, and the experience as the children of Ishmael. Still she sat waiting while the sounds, the accumulating voltages loose and wheeling in the air, arranged themselves toward that instant perfect pattern point. The audience below her was a restless shifting multitude in the gloom—a conglomerate of all the Arab world, fluid Saudi head drapery and Tunisian turbans and sober European suits, with here and there a pale moth glow of white veils where brides were sitting with their grooms on their wedding night. Across this throng passed intermittent

37

participatory shivers, amazed approving *Ahhhhhhs* at certain turns and hoverings in the sounds from the stage. The air sweltered. Cats coiled up and down the aisles. At the slightest gesture from Oum Kalsoum, the faintest intimation that she might be preparing to stand and sing, there was a general vast shuddering over the hall, a scatter of gasps, and when she suddenly cocked her head downward once after an especially close and tantalizing pass by the moment of truth, it brought a huge convulsive groan, with one man finally lunging to his feet and whooping entreaties to her until those around him frantically waved and whispered him back down. "There are one hundred million people listening to her at this moment," Fawzi whispered, "on radios all the way from Algeria to Oman. Myself, it sends a tingling up my spine every time. I cannot help it."

But to the American the bursts of appreciative applause, the transported yowls always came at an unexpected moment, slightly startling him, as if there were proceeding in this hall some interplay in a different psychic language, the indecipherable spiritual code of an alien sensibility. And at last, unfurling her scarf with a shake of her hand, she arose. There was a long release, an explosion of bellows, cheers, clapping. She waited until it subsided, and then, almost stealthily, her voice began—a winding wobbling wail, a sound like some fluting that had filtered down through the centuries from the gardens of Ur, the fierce plains of the Hittites, Babylon, Nineveh, Thebes, and having to do with the unutterably sweet anguish that is the Arab understanding of love: seeming, to the American, somewhat curious in translation ("Oh, I still want you, the man I have lost. . . . I want to tell you of the fire of my love. . . . I want you, the man who will not let me sleep the whole night. . . . I want to photograph you. . . .") but never-theless sending pulses of ecstasy through the hall, releasing at points a berserk caterwauling that sounded like a whole back yard full of lovelorn cats, people erupting from their seats all around, white-robed Yemenites and capped Sudanese, to shake their arms heavenward like a faith healer's tent meeting, some of them finally running down the aisle, shouting to her, unable to bear it, until with the slightest flick of her scarf she shooed them, reeling, back to their seats. Men, after lighting cigarettes, were putting out match flames with slow gentle pinches of their fingers. "This is fantastic," the American whispered to Fawzi. He noticed then that Lani had moved to the top step of the aisle before them, sitting there now alone as she listened, her back to them, her face hidden, her shoulders slightly hunched forward, hugging herself.

It was still proceeding when, sometime after one in the morning, they made their way back down the alley to the night club, where their voices were slower and quieter. Lani sat for a while, slumped on a stool with her back to the bar, lost now in Lethean fogs through which she peered at the others around her. "Look at us," she said suddenly. "Nobody in this place cares about anything—no one is serious. We don't belong anywhere—not to the past, not to the present, not to the future. So we live like this every night. But the problem is you wake up in the morning in a different world, you have to go to work and face people who are different from you. They are so serious. . . ."

But beyond all his sessions with those daytime people in the plaster geometric buildings—the bureaucrats of the revolu-tion in their plain dark suits, earnestly and meticulously assembling a reality out of statistics and Marxist dogmas and U.N. resolutions over endless servings of lemonade and hot tea and coffee, while he listened and tidily sipped in distracted attentiveness to his own uneasy truce with his lower digestive system—he was beginning to think he detected something oddly and furtively familiar about the place. He experienced at times the fleeting sensation—perhaps it was in the weather, he thought—of having slipped into the comfortable accustomed sags of an old sweater.

When he had landed at the Cairo airport, he had seen a group of Arabs at one end of the waiting room—men with sluggish heavy sun-parched faces, in dusty drooping khaki trousers and black serge coats and open-collared plain shirts, pinching in their horny hands the smoldering stubs of cigarettes—who could have passed with their white head drapery for a delegation of back-country Mississippi deputy sheriffs or a collection of South Georgia tobacco farmers sitting around a courthouse square on a Saturday afternoon with handkerchiefs over their heads in the heat. A few days after he arrived, he passed a long and pleasant afternoon with the family of the Egyptian couple he had met back in Atlanta, having delivered a pressure cooker the wife had given him for her father. They were all gathered in an uncle's apartment at the top of a Cairo tenement, in a small high-ceilinged front parlor rather cramped with an abundance of formal Victorian furniture under gilt-scrolled picture frames that seemed to have been translated from some more expansive fine room into these contracted spaces. The apartment was filled now with kinfolk who kept replenishing themselves in a seemingly unending series of shifts from a hall outside, so that he never quite got them counted: a stationary gallery of grandmothers and aunts ranged along the far wall, their stockinged ample ankles crossed and their hands nestled in their laps, faces talcumed in the heat with tiny mustaches of perspiration on upper lips, their hair in buns with only a few stray frizzles at the temples; along with a twisty little boy in crisp seersucker pajamas apparently just awakened from his nap; a dark glistening plum of a daughter just emerged surprised and blushing from childhood; the inevitable manless old woman, spinster or long-widowed, tucked off in a corner partially hidden by a pink satin lampshade, who wanted to know immediately, "America or Egypt—which better?" and then remained silent for the rest of the time, merely nodding now and then in approbation from her corner as she listened to the others talk. Any mention of politics, the war— any unpleasantness whatsoever—was daintily avoided. The conversation was devoted to the couple back in Atlanta— those distant cherished children—and when he happened once to mention the husband's name, one of the women along the wall crossed her plump arms and shook her head from side to side, her eyes presently brimming, and then abruptly arose and withdrew from the room, somewhat embarrassing the others. "She misses her son very much," the uncle explained sotto voce with an apologetic smile, "so that you only have to say his name and she begins to cry, she cannot help it." *By God, what good people,* he thought. *What truly good, unnoticed people there are all over this world. God bless these people. . . .* He found tea, cake, ice cream, coffee appearing before him in unbroken succession—indeed, had the sense of being some rare *caller*—while, all through that long polite ceremonious old-fashioned afternoon, a soft hot wind breathed into the room through slow soundless furls of white lace curtains in the open window.

41

It was, in essence, a classic Southern afternoon. Indeed, as it began to turn out, Egypt is not all that alien to a Southerner: in *The Earl of Louisiana,* A. J. Liebling proposes that the states of Deepest Dixie—Louisiana, Mississippi, a bit of Alabama, and a bit of Texas—are merely a continuation of a single long cultural littoral which also encompasses such Mediterranean societies as Egypt and Algeria and Lebanon, that the Mediterranean and Caribbean and Gulf of Mexico "form a homogeneous though interrupted sea." There had always seemed a certain style of voluptuousness among the Texas baronies that reminded him of oil sheikdoms along the Persian Gulf, as if there is some common efflorescence to societies that dwell on the marge of enclosed seas. Beyond so much obsessive coffee-drinking (Turkish coffee, which is both sipped and gently chewed) in so much heat, he felt himself in a culture which—like the South until recently, at least—still belonged more to the earth than to machines (it occurred to him he had even taken the same inoculations that probably would have been necessary if he had been traveling, say, back to the South before the New Deal, when it was still largely a gullied land of pellagra and trichinosis and malaria), a people who had remained in a kind of historical ennui, a society fundamentally and abidingly inert rather than kinetic, but in which there is a feverish and lavish private play of energies, an old-fashioned sentimentality, a quick combustibility of temperament, and a sense of identity and loyalty beginning with one's immediate neighborhood and then proceeding in ever-diminishing priorities outward: "The truth is, I'm afraid," one Egyptian government official told him, "the Arab world will never really unite. They have a way of maintaining this appearance for the outside world of an extraordinary courtesy and graciousness, but they still don't have any larger sense of community than that of a tribe. They only cohere in a crisis"—a condition reminiscent of the states of the Confederacy.

Nevertheless, they cultivate civility of a gallantry, sometimes almost intimidating, that approaches the heroic. Letters from the Egyptian couple in Atlanta had preceded him to Cairo, and one evening not long after he arrived, he was visited by a younger brother of the wife's, answering the faint uncertain tapping at the door of his hotel room and ushering the youth on inside where he then seemed to dangle in some strange and helpless distraction, suffering repeated hopeless breakdowns in his English, elaborately grinning and bobbing up again and again from his chair. Presently, there came another brief light tapping at the door, and, opening it, he discovered a friend of the brother's who, unseen when the brother was admitted, had simply been standing patiently alone out in the hall for a full five minutes. This friend of the brother, Yousry, later accompanied the American to the Pyramids—so do cordial associations in Egypt infinitely proliferate—and toward the end of the afternoon, turning once to find Yousry placing a coin in the palm of a man who had lifted a wire to let them pass onto the ground around the Sphinx, he realized that for the past two hours Yousry had been quietly making such tips behind his back. Later, when he had been let out back at the hotel, he glanced behind him as he entered the lobby to see Yousry now engaged in some fitful exchange with the cabdriver that seemed only an instant away from blows —and it struck him how desperately spare, financially, Yousry no doubt actually was, how many silent little inward nips of despair he had suffered through that afternoon as he parted again and again with coins behind this American's oblivious back—yet continuing on, not even tabulating after a while the inexorable accumulation of this private disaster, in simple fidelity to a relentless discipline of graciousness to the point where, finally on his own again, faced with yet another tip, he had to salvage what he could at the risk of an actual physical fight.

The fact is, though, all confrontations in Egypt tend finally to wind up histrionic rather than physical transactions. With a compulsive inflationary extravagance of rhetoric, they conscientiously sustain the sweet wiles that dreams can exercise against the present: they have, of course, an old and complex wisdom about mirages. As a result, for them, rhetoric has a way of effectively replacing reality, a constant sleight of hand that has been going on for centuries until it seems no longer discernible. Perhaps for that reason, the persistent small suggestions he met everywhere that he might be a C.I.A. agent began to have on him a Kafkaesque effect; after a while, he began to *feel* like one, even began at moments answering and relating like one. But neither was this an unfamiliar alchemy: it has long been the disposition of the South to invest in words the intensity, the consequence, the life of a reality dispelling the insupportable one at hand, and words having been taken with such seriousness, indeed with such passion—because they have always counted for more there than elsewhere— may be one reason the South since Reconstruction has been so lush with writers.

As he was to discover later, the Israelis have at least an academic and somewhat bemused understanding of this instinct in their adversaries. "The Arabs simply don't like people who only want to tell the truth," one Israeli minister told him. "Such an attitude is subversive to them, such a man is dangerous in some way. This is true even of the most sophisticated Arabs

—they will be quite realistic with you individually, but when they are together, imagination takes over. There is a favorite Arab story of mine about this sheik who was sitting under a tree, smoking his hubble-bubble, when some children around him began making a terrible noise with their play. So he thinks, I must find some way to get rid of this awful noise, and he calls them over and tells them, 'What are you doing here; did not you know that Old Auntie is distributing candy at the other end of the village?' The children got very excited then and ran off toward the other end of the village, leaving the old sheik in peace again under his tree. But after a few minutes had passed, he began to reflect, What am I doing sitting here? Those children are going to get all that candy—what about me?" Another Israeli official in the foreign ministry admitted, "We know there is a big difference between words and actual action in the Arab world. The problem is wishful thinking has a way of becoming fact for them. They convince themselves with their rhetoric. I have an Arab friend who was telling me once that all the Arabs are confident Israel intends to establish this empire over all of Mesopotamia, and I asked him, 'But surely you do not believe in such a fantastic idea?' and he told me, 'What do you mind if I believe in it? It *pleases* me to believe in it.'"

Perhaps accordingly, the events that fill this separate cosmos of rhetoric—speeches opening new fronts, reiterations of positions launching new offenses, ultimatums that corner and cut off the enemy, all the pronouncements that await only the petty vulgarity of taking place are elaborately and solemnly reported on Cairo's radio and in the newspapers. Oratory makes serious news. Occassional interventions of brute empirical facts—like the defeat of 1967—are not so much positive incursions of reality as great capricious nihilistic sucks from space creating momentary voids and vacuums which rhetoric, declarations, proclamations rush to fill, to reconstruct the wreckage. The truth is Egyptian press officials seem innocently incapable of understanding a visiting journalist's interest in anything beyond official explanations of political positions, accounts of events, and field displays of those accounts—any other curiosity strikes them as irrelevant and eccentric, if not incipiently anarchistic. Needless to say, this is a presumption about news which Western journalists find infernally difficult, and they soon resign themselves to operating obliquely, a recourse in which those journalists who dealt with officials in Southern towns during the classic Southern decade of the Negro Awakening eventually became practiced. Actually, according to one Egyptian government functionary, "the people only believe, say, fifty percent of what they read and hear on the radio. If you want to know, they are very worried, at times, deep down, about Israel. But while they may believe only fifty percent, it's a different fifty percent depending on the circumstances." It's as if they all are immobilized in some twilight zone between these furtive cynicisms and the general anesthesia of a total credulity. In any event, propaganda is really everything, it remains the only true reality, which somewhat explains the government's particularly grim preoccupation with press matters. While in Cairo, the American paid one visit to the press building, and after filing with others past security guards checking identification cards, he entered a low lobby of marbled floors and pillars resembling a newly renovated bus terminal, only its corridors and mezzanine were extravagantly sandbagged, soldiers scowling over these fortifications with submachine guns and rifles.

With their sense of reality, then, forever a shadow rear-ranging itself after the rhetoric—evanescence, which among other things considerably unsettles the Israelis contemplating even official Arab recognition of their existence as a state—they have summoned forth since 1967 a kind of Battle of Britain vision of their situation, a vision which assumed an instant and utter plausibility retroactively encompassing all that went before, and in which they now enjoy, refreshingly, more moral persuasion than was ever theirs before. This has been, in fact, one of 1967's backfire gifts to them. "It's to be or not to be," they insist with absolute sincerity. "We don't have any other alternative but to resist Israel. It's our existence, our future." As one Egyptian official explained with the same complete ingenuousness, "I know that we have said at times in the past things about driving people into seas, such things, but of course you understand that in a situation of grave crisis and danger, you have to say certain things just to keep up the morale, the confidence of your people. But truthfully, now—of *course*, we have accepted the existence of the Jewish state. I mean, after all, twenty years have now passed: whether we may like it or not, Israel is a fact. Check the statements since 1967, and you will find there is nothing in our recipe about pushing Israel into the sea, any such business as that. Why, by our acceptance simply of the '67 U.N. resolution, which itself presumes the fact of the state of Israel, we have already tacitly recognized and accepted Israel's existence. No, that is not the problem. You must understand that the problem is simply Israel occupying the territory of Egypt, which she took from Egypt in aggressive war—and of course, the problem, the original problem of the Palestinians; think of this entire dispossessed people and you will see what we are talking about, which I will be frank to admit, yes, we did not start to realize was the real problem ourselves until 1967." (Some weeks later, in a remarkable interview on the NET forum "The Advocates," Nasser—only about three months before his death —serenely repeated substantively the same thing, the interviewer stumbling somewhat incredulously, did he understand him right, was he actually saying—and Nasser, with his dark moist eyes batting almost shyly and a steady vaguely embarrassed little smile fixed under his tiny dapper mustache, insisting, yes, yes—not only did Egypt accept the existence of Israel, but with an evacuation of Egyptian territory Egypt would even guarantee the integrity of Israel against harassments by Palestinian guerrillas from Egypt's side. It was a boggling profession which, for the rest of that show and the weeks that followed, was simply left in the air, as if it could not be assimilated.)

Indeed, behind all their ferocious public posturing, he could not escape the suspicion that they were, personally, an incorrigibly gentle folk. The military governor who had addressed the journalists in the bunker at Suez—beginning, "I wish to say to you that I send my greetings to the people you are coming from . . ."—seemed, in the midst of all that elemental savage wreckage, an outrageously misplaced and cherubic man, as bland and butter-soft, with his sweetheart eyes and lambent rose-petal Gerber-baby skin, as some organist for an Episcopal church choir. His impression lingered that, in some profound way, they were not comfortable with the actual final physical business of violence; the guards at the airports, at the public buildings, all had some slight air of gruff abashment and awkwardness inside their lethal regalia, seemed studiously trying to maintain their appearance of fearsomeness. At the Cairo airport as he was waiting for his flight to Amman, he saw a group of young army recruits huddled closely together at the end of the terminal, country youths clumsily holding official forms to which they seemed to have become suddenly stuck as to flypaper, and casting about them now stares of uncomprehending hopelessness. And there seemed an almost touchingly homemade and makeshift look to much of their military equipment, with rudely hand-painted insignias on the cabs of their trucks and half-tracks. The security signs at military installations—"Don't Believe Rumors," "Watch Out, Someone Is Overlistening"—were reminiscent of those flat simple childlike drawings on the walls of the tombs, the figures simply translated now into business suits of emerald-green and wine and purple like characters in comic-book illustrations. During the raid at Suez, a group of soldiers, noticing suddenly that a television camera had paused on them, immediately and instinctively assembled themselves into a slightly grandiloquent arrangement of poses, faces grave and lifted, weapons all held at conspicuous and somewhat theatrical angles of readiness, suggesting somehow an old tintype of Mexican bandits pausing for their portrait in a palmed and wallpapered photographer's parlor. "The truth is," an official in one Western embassy allowed, "the Egyptians simply don't like to fight, God bless them. Why, during the campaign in Yemen, their fighter pilots would get out of radar range and dump their bombs in empty wadis and fly around a little bit and then come zooming back into their bases with bomb bays empty and reports of terrific destruction. It's not really a matter of fear, it's just that, when you come right down to it, Egyptians do not like to kill. There's no way to understand them unless you understand that." There is the impression that if they finally must kill, their impulse is to get it done and finished as quickly, completely, and impersonally as possible, hopefully by means of technical devices with the area of fatal application as far removed from their immediate vicinity as possible: in a certain sense, this would even explain their occasional use of gas in the Yemeni campaign.

An Arab driver with whom the American rode frequently was fond of dredging forth jokes for his amusement whenever there was a light and relaxed moment: "You know what is the camel with no hump? Make a guess. You cannot guess? The answer is Hubert Humphrey. Heh. See? Hump-*free*. I know another one. What is a Negro who bathes in the Red Sea? A Negro who bathes in the Red Sea is wet. You do not get it? You don't like jokes? Maybe you like instead to be serious all the time. . . ." In defense, then, the American mustered the riddle of the little moron tiptoeing past the medicine cabinet. A look of critical bafflement seized the driver's face, until he told him, "He didn't want to wake up the sleeping pills." The driver pondered a moment, "He didn't want to wake—" and then boomed, "Ahhh. Oh, no—oh, hah-hah-hah," his laughter lasting him, in repeating delicious blasts of delight, for the next three miles, while his passenger speculated on the difficulty of accepting the fabled bloodthirstiness of a people with such a sense of humor. There were times when it seemed they were merely engaged in a fierce grimacing and gesticulation and breast-beating to exorcise some demon—histrionics to which, before very long, they find themselves nevertheless committed. Possibly this made for a kind of dangerous duality in their nature, an emotional dubiousness which produced a certain constant high nervousness with implications of a hovering hysteria peculiarly troubling and exhausting to Westerners.

When he had first landed at the Cairo airport, the cab had carried him into town past countless identical peeling posters left from the visit weeks before of the current President of another African Socialist republic. And then it came to him, fully stunned him as they passed a looming billboard on which Lenin was stiffly extending a burning torch into a heroic bloody sky, that he was suddenly in the hands of strangers. He later found the informal diplomatic mission that the United States still maintains in Egypt, but it was merely a rather haggard and scantily populated little outpost disguised as the Spanish Embassy, and the only American functionary he came across there was the political officer, a slight bespectacled man a bit crinkled and damp in the heat who suggested a divinity student in some Midwestern fundamentalist seminary or a junior accountant in some vast insurance company; it was not inconceivable that the fate of the planet could depend at some moment on how excellently this modest and inauspicious figure exercised his art.

But on his first night in Cairo, as he was sitting alone by the window of a supper club atop a hotel overlooking the Nile, he found his state of vertigo only complicated when, like some sourceless woof and feedback of the land he had left far behind, the band suddenly began playing Grand Ole Opry country and Western numbers—"Donnn't forget . . . to reee-member me" —followed by hard-wheeling rock music with the true gut sound of jukeboxes in all-night truck stops in Tifton, Georgia, or Ennis, Texas, and finally, improbably, with the Nile a soft continuous mercurial wrinkling of reflections below him in the musky Egyptian night, they rendered that humid old gospel hymn out of the pine-plank country churches and sawdust tent revivals of his boyhood: "Oh, Happy Day! . . . When Jeees-sus! washed my sins away. . . ." And he felt then an almost strangling flush of unsuspected submerged tenderness for the States, thinking, *So I love it after all; at such moments one cannot help loving it,* presently ordering another bottle of wine as his astonished spirit, from this distance now of six thousand miles, like the Ancient Mariner giddily opened and embraced all of his country indiscriminately, its dauntless vicious ugliness as well as all its good homespun naïve beauties, all its ebullient vulgarities and generosities, its staggering presumption and ambition. He privately celebrated now atop this hotel overlooking the Nile: *Incredible. Their diplomacy might belong to Russia, but their heart, by God, belongs to us. So boorish, and blundering and pious—how the hell did we do it? But there's news for Wendell Willkie, no doubt about it: it's become one world, and its secret name is America; it speaks in a universal tongue of Burt Bacharach and Warner Brothers and Marlboros, Park Avenue and Times Square and Sunset Boulevard, along with Dodge City and The Ponderosa, General Motors and Kodak and Procter & Gamble: it's one world, and it's "The Ed Sullivan Show".* . . . Somewhat later in the evening, a more or less authentic Egyptian belly dancer materialized—a woman ripened to a rather extravagant sumptuousness with a faint vaccination dent on her left thigh—who shortly produced, among the tables of assorted Egyptian establishment dignitaries around her, the whoops and brays and table whackings of a troupe of Terre Haute Shriners on convention in St. Louis, and watching them he fancied Sinclair Lewis in Italy suddenly realizing he was lonesome for George Babbitt, discovering he loved Gopher Prairie. (But the next morning he found, among the wire copy that had spilled in overnight onto the floor of the government press building, a vague and spidery carbon of the report of the killings at Kent State, and in that sudden bleak wash of disappointment and emptiness and confusion that had become a not unfamiliar sensation of late back in his country, it seemed possible that the United States was merely communicating its most meaningless scintillations to the rest of the world, which the world was witlessly absorbing —less America's triumph than Madison Avenue's—while the nation itself was in the throes of struggling still with its own dim deepest truths.)

Nevertheless, he began to sense some beginning schizophrenias in the life of Egypt now. Although he continued to come across private hankerings after the West and particularly the United States (in the entrance of one nightspot along the Nile called The Salt and Pepper Club, there were pop posters of Steve McQueen and Lee Marvin and The Jefferson Airplane, while on the floor Egyptian youths were snapping and pumping to an organ and electric guitar in swooping flares of colored lights), he sat through a succession of interviews in which Egyptian officials kept pointing out with incensed airs that Israel was an American imperialist intrusion, an alien Western presence artificially introduced into the Middle Eastern culture: "Golda Meir, what does she understand of this part of the world?" one of them clipped. "She was born in Russia, she taught school in Minneapolis, U.S.A.; what is she doing over here now among the Arabs, I ask you?" An editor at the government newspaper, *Al Ahram*—a trim taut somewhat fastidious man in a drab brown suit whose office shelves contained, along with the selected works of Mao Tse-tung, *LBJ Country* and Evans and Novak's *Lyndon B. Johnson: The Exercise of Power* —briskly asserted, "It is quite clear Palestine was chosen by the West as a political foothold for their interests in this part of the world. Why else is there this foreign state in our midst? Why should it be the Arabs who have to pay for what Hitler did to the Jews? Israel was put here, obviously, to constitute a cen-

53

tral block to Arab unity. How could we ever achieve unity now with Israel in the middle? She would never leave us in peace, she would never allow it." (Besides Israel, at least one other difficulty that has so far sabotaged all prospects of unity is what one Egyptian official described as "our Pharaoh complex. We still believe we are just a little better than anyone else, which is why we've never really gotten along with the rest of Arabs, why none of the Arabs like us—this was the problem finally in that business with Syria a while ago: they just didn't want to be an Egyptian province.")

But while they are now studiously maintaining an official estrangement from the West, it seems somehow a faintly reluctant and wistful alienation. A man who designed one of Cairo's more handsome and habitable official buildings—a fifty-eight-year-old entrepreneur whose family fortune was assimilated by the revolution but whose services continue to be quietly enlisted by the government, while he cheerfully advertises himself still as "an unreconstructed capitalist, I can't help it, I'm too old to change now"—exuberantly declared one morning, "Look, now, everything in this building I put up—*everything,* I tell you, from the telephones to the girders to the chair you're sitting on—is all from the West. Nothing from Russia, absolutely nothing from the East—except, wait a minute, excuse me, the doorknobs, yes, they're from China, but only because I happened to come across them for a very reasonable price." Even government officials, in the American's conversations with them, seemed always careful to mention that "most of our new generation coming up, you know, is still schooled in the West!" According to reports there, even the brother of Hassanein Heikel, who was Nasser's closest confidant and the editor of *Al Ahram,* is studying "on a campus out somewhere, I believe, in your Texas."

The only remotely Russian beguilement he came across in Egypt, in fact, was one number played by the band at the hotel on the Nile: the theme from *Dr. Zhivago*. Frequently he would step into hotel elevators to find American oilmen there talking in Texas whangs: "Tried my luck for several hours last night in that casino of theirs downstairs, but I quit twenty bucks ahead. . . ." Indeed, one Cairo public figure demanded somewhat plaintively, "What is wrong with the United States— doesn't it realize there are one hundred million Arabs just dying to become a part of the West? What the hell do we have in common with the Russians? This is one of the craziest marriages in the history of diplomatic alliances, but what goddam choice have you given us? Egypt has said to the United States, we've done nothing against you, we've bent over backward trying to accommodate you, and all you've done is slap us in the face. So our agreement with the Russians is hardly a matter of ideology —how can you say it's ideology when we have thousands of Communists in Egyptian jails? It's purely a matter of national interests—an arrangement of convenience on the part of the Russians, an arrangement of desperation on our part. We're under no illusions about the Russians, believe me—you think we don't know they're playing football with us? We're caught in the gears, that's all. I'll tell you, we don't even get along with them very well. The people in the streets, they just don't like them. Maybe it's because, you know, they seem so serious, so dull and so—what's the word?—*severe*, so severe, and people get the idea they're tight about their money; they don't tip, you know. But when the Russians go out shopping, the butchers won't even sell them anything, believe me, they spit on them. The Russians hate it here, there's no doubt about that. It drives them crazy, this treatment. They buy something, the people in the shops just throw it at them on the counter. Really, this is bad, it's got to stop somehow. After all, they *are* helping us here enormously. . . ."

But one Western professor in a Cairo university even proposes, "Egypt, if you can believe it, tacitly recognizes that the United States has to be around to balance off the Russians, to keep this country from falling completely into the Russian's sphere." They are purportedly more scrupulous about associations with Red China; after the battle of Shadwan Island, in which Israel actually made off with a complete Egyptian radar station, China reportedly sent Egypt a note saying no nation should be humiliated that way, with the implication that China would assist Egypt in insuring it would never happen again— a note which Nasser promptly took to Moscow and flourished before the Russians, supposedly precipitating the present Russian commitment in Egypt. But still one rarely glimpses Russians on the streets in Cairo. More or less by the mutual consent of both governments, Russian personnel and advisers are kept carefully secluded in their compounds and barracks—in part a precaution of the Soviets, so rumor has it, to keep their people insulated from the covert Western blandishments and treacherous Babylonian pipings still profusely at play in the streets. One newspaperman recently in Alexandria reported that Russian sailors on shore leave there proceed from their ship through the city and then back to their ship marched by an officer in a precise squad formation.

While he was at the Giza Pyramids, the American came across a Russian family trudging down the short dirt road to the Sphinx—a large outing, including not only a generous brood of children but also, it seemed, a collection of great-aunts and grandmothers, who all had a look as plain and sturdy as potatoes and could have been a vacationing Iowa family on a brief hasty expedition through Juárez, sunless and flushed and sowewhat displaced in their tourist trappings of sunglasses and aqua shorts and cameras and wide-brimmed hats. Almost as if by some signal, a dozen or so small boys, waifs, appeared along the banks on each side of them, flickering over the rocks like salamanders for a few seconds and then beginning to filter one by one down into the road to ask the family for coins. After a moment, there was an urgent approaching hammer of hoofs coming down the hill, and an Egyptian horseman swept by, scattering the waifs back up into the rocks, wheeling his horse and lunging part of the way up the bank after them in a clacking and shaling of rubble, continuing to keep them at a distance until the Russians, who trudged on with only one or two bemused glances at this Cossack-like operation around them, reached the Sphinx at the bottom of the hill.

He began to suspect that—behind all the fierce fulminations, the grim gesturing, the formal rationales, the official compendiums of outrages, the diplomatic chronologies and genealogies, the intricate political astrology charts, the whole long grave ponderous mummery of U.N. resolutions and withdrawn ambassadors and official ultimatums—there was actually something else going on, some profound national trauma involved, arising out of an immense and complicated accident of history. Since 1948, these ancient people, still dazed with God and the old murmurings of the earth, have found themselves next to a society manufactured instant and whole out of the twentieth century, a quick complete functioning technological and scientific order, externally contrived and installed now in their immediate neighborhood and therefore necessarily altering their own measure of themselves. The fact is Israel poses—not only to Egypt but to much of the rest of the Arab world—a deep and massive

affront, intimidation, outrage. The original crisis in the encounter between Israel and the Arabs has not been the balance
of power, but, for the Arabs, that balance of communal com-
parison—the community of intimate proximities—which makes
up one's sense of identity and well-being.

There are still Arab leaders who insist the Jews simply cannot fight: one Western embassy official recalled, "I had an Arab
military man approach me once and implore me to arrange for
the Arabs to win just one battle—'It does not have to be an
important one,' he said, 'just one battle, that's all we need, and
after that reality will be set straight again.'" In their almost
panicky bombasts against the prospect of the delivery of more
Phantom jets to Israel, they seemed to betray a peculiar almost
mystical reverence for the ultimate efficacy of technology. It's
as if all their frustrations reduce to a simple matter of equipment,
hardware; the answers for how it has all happened lie in
mechanical devices. They seem to have a particular naïve awe
for the witchcraft of American machines: "Anything American,"
said one veteran diplomat to the Middle East, "they regard as
traveling first class. Nothing can touch American technology.
Those Phantoms, you know, they just never miss—though the
MIGs Egypt has are really about as capable." All this, then,
merely amplifies their genuine phobia about Israel, which has
come into possession of all this magic. American technology has
become equivalent to the supernatural rod of Moses: again and
again, it has brought the Red Sea closing over them. It should
be accepted that, in regard to Israel, Egypt has passed now
directly and completely from the policies of pursuit to the
perspectives of paranoia—a paranoia, actually, that would be
hard to exaggerate. One Egyptian government figure earnestly
explained, "Did you know that, right now, at this minute, the

Israelis have no official map of their country? That's right, they
have nothing whatsoever showing the actual boundaries of
Israel. You must understand, the ambitions of the Jews are endless. Not only would they like a nation extending from the Nile
to the Euphrates, but their ambitions extend even to having a
President in the White House." More than once, Egyptian officials invoked the American colonial crime of the pioneers and
the Indians: "They want to do to us precisely what the United
States did to the Indians. Their cavalry comes and takes our
land, and then they move their settlers in. It is the same thing
exactly." They seemed to repeat almost obsessively, "We are
aware of what the Jews think of us, yes. They look on us as
half savages. We are half civilized, yes, and the only way to
deal with us is force, that's all we understand." One Arab
professor in Amman later told the American, "Look back in the
scriptures, if you will: what were the instructions Joshua received
from Jehovah before the invasion—destroy everything, kill men,
women, and children, spare nothing. You think they have
changed? This has been their history. . . ."

At the same time, it has seemed to be their response to
cultivate a studied distaste and resentment of the Western
mentality of Israel—the brisk assertiveness, the impatience with
amenities—which accost, as they put it, Arab sensibilities. As
one Arab leader said with a sniff, "You take an Arab and an
Israeli standing before a beautiful cascade. The Arab would
immediately begin trying to compose a poem about it, but the
Israeli would say, 'Now, how can I use this to electrify a town?' "
While the American was in Egypt, he attended a lecture at a
Cairo university—held in a chamber like a peacock-jeweled royal
Persian palace room—and with the golden afternoon outside
slowly extinguishing into a lavender twilight, the speaker mused,

"Westerners know with the eye, and thereby the brain. But it has always been the way of the African to know with the touch, the skin, the heart." An Egyptian government spokesman later told the American, "You see, the problem with Israel is that it acts out of the Western mind. They want something hastily, would win it with battles. They think only of operating in the practical circumstances of the moment, that is the trouble."

But the culture shock seems to be that they finally know, in their heart of hearts, that they have not been able to prevail over Israel precisely because Israel is more Western than they: that, by some mischievous machination of history, to defeat Israel, even to cope with her, Egypt would, in some essential sense, have to cease being Egypt, have to finally not survive. It is no surprise, then, that he came across occasional hints of a deep and brooding malaise of spirit, a vast private weather of inadequacy and enervation and weariness. An American newspaperman he met in Cairo told him of a conversation with an Egyptian commercial pilot in a bar: "I asked him after a while, 'Just why the hell is it, now, that the Israelis keep shooting down your planes all the time? I mean, you know and I know these MIGs aren't all that inferior to Phantoms, so why is it?' and this guy says, 'Do I really have to answer that? It's finally the difference between their pilots and ours. It only takes an Israeli pilot about a year to reach the level of efficiency, effectiveness that it takes our pilots three, four, five years to reach.' So I said, 'But why should that be? I mean, is the training—' and this Egyptian says, 'Look, I don't know. It just seems we lack the mental acumen the Israelis have, that's all.' "

Late one afternoon, as he was sitting with a group of government officials and doctors and architects around a lawn table at the Gezira Club, one of them suddenly announced after a silence, his voice small and quiet and abstract in the gathering dusk with dim glimmers of white gnats hanging over the golf green around him, "You know, sometimes you can't help but get the feeling we just don't belong in this century. Every now and then, I just get this feeling we aren't at home, we're lost in this time. . . ."

But while they are locked in an ambivalence that acts at once to absolve and to exalt the failures it insures, there remains still in their nature that final precipitate readiness to place the matter of one's pride against all profit: an implacable willingness to eat one's liver for the sake of an Arab kind of machismo. The difficulty for the West and for Israel is its instinct to deal with things as they are: what matters at the beginning in the Middle East is dealing with things as the other side *thinks* they are—and for Egypt, at least, whatever have been its blusters and fantasies in the past, it has become simply a question of getting its name back. And it was Nasser who, alone, personified this promise for them.

In the end, this was Nasser's meaning to the Egyptians—in him they found for the first time in centuries some promise of getting back their name. His conspicuous practical failures, both at home and against the confoundment of Israel, were not really relevant. After Egypt's disaster in the Six-Day War and his announced resignation, the improbable spectacle of their massive popular clamor for him to remain in office, partially induced but also largely spontaneous, was a celebration of the man impervious to the catastrophe he had led them into, almost as if he had endeared himself more to them by defeat than he could have by actual triumph. To the Israelis, of course, those demonstrations were simple proof of the impossible perversity of the Arab mind. Though at his death he had not really impinged any more than superficially on his people's ancient condition of abjectness, still—if only by contrast to the gaudily corrupt figure of King Farouk before him—he had become for most of them a folk hero. Whatever his diplomatic duplicities, they seemed to sense in this withdrawn soft-spoken abstemious man, at least, a certain personal decency and piety and a passionate fidelity to the interests of Egypt after a long season of colonial pillage and venality. He was the best thing they had been given for a long time. His name was daily on their breath, became almost as intimate to them as the name of Egypt itself. The abrupt loss of such a folk leader—such a deprivation by fate—is finally more calamitous to a society like Egypt's than any defeat by alien armies, alien technologies.

But his departure, the American speculated from the States, would not necessarily bode well for Israel. Leadership in the Arab world tends now to amount to a competition of enmity against Israel, and it was hard to imagine anything emerging from the struggle of successors in Egypt other than, at least for a time, a deeper implacability. Beyond that, even while he was in Egypt, it seemed to the American they had already retreated finally to their old immemorial reliance—time. As a last recourse against their adversaries, Egypt has used time as the Russians have used geography. "The Crusaders were here for two hundred years, but finally they left," asserted one Egyptian intellectual. "The Turks were here for four hundred years—where are they now? Today it is Israel. We are patient. We know how to wait." It could be pointed out, of course, that the Jews turned in a fairly respectable two-thousand-year feat of patience themselves. But more importantly, in the terms of Egypt's need now, victory and defeat lose all their common meaning: all the normal measures of defeat—wars that come to disaster, wide devastations of properties and resources, occupations—become merely bad accidents. Indeed, in this context victory and defeat lose *all* effective meaning, since they lie indefinitely removed from the actual experience of lifetimes or even generations.

At Suez, after the bombing raid had passed, he and the other foreign journalists were collected together again and taken by car several blocks through the empty wreckage to an alleyway where they found a gathering of men, all wearing dark green militia uniforms, clustered at the blank end of the alley under balconies sagging from the gutted roofless stumps of buildings. With the opening of the car doors, they erupted into wild and ecstatic music, a slapping of drums and clapping shouting chants over the savage wavering wail of a crude stringed instrument fingered by an old man who had the fogged faded eyes of the blind. Suddenly one youth leaped forward and began an oddly formal stamping dance, heels kicking behind him like Spanish flamenco flourishes, while the others now clapped him on raptly, almost amorously, chanting as he would crouch with a skyward gaze and then lunge forward, flinging his arm, the others shouting while someone translated for the journalists: "No, no, America, don't give planes to Israel. . . . Go tell Nasser we love him, we will fight for him forever. . . ." At the least, the American thought, it was no inconsiderable stroke of superb theatre; they are beginning to develop a fine sense of stage work. As he watched it, he thought of a passage from George Steiner's *The Death of Tragedy:* "*. . . Perhaps, tragedy has merely altered in style and convention. . . . I have seen a documentary film showing the activities of a Chinese agricultural commune. . . . They formed into a large chorus and began chanting a song of hatred against China's foes. Then a group leader leapt from the*

63

ranks and performed a kind of violent, intricate dance. He was acting out in pantomime the struggle against the imperialist bandits and their defeat by the peasant armies. The ceremony closed with a recital of the heroic death of one of the founders of the local Communist party. . . . Is it not, I wonder, in some comparable rite of defiance and honor to the dead that tragedy began, three thousand years ago, on the plains of Arges?"

But the disquieting difference is that such rites involve mere formidable complications now. The morning that he left Egypt —as he was passing beyond that palmed suburb of tapioca-yellow stucco villas and lipstick-crimson flowers on out into the treeless expanse of sand stenciled with barbed wire and guard towers before they reached the airport—there suddenly appeared from a side road a caravan of five long flat-bed trailer trucks, their cabs painted the color of spoiled mayonnaise, each of them bearing the enormous reclining netted shape of a Russian missile. What kind of massive brutish insanity is at work, he thought, that has managed to strategically implicate the destiny of the world in the broodings and deliriums of these haggard and dusty backlands of history? But then, he speculated, it is probably always unsettling to an American to discover he may actually be critically and finally involved in deadly peeves and confusions and malevolences transpiring far from the inviolate shores of his own country's experience—Americans probably still remain in the deep center of their hearts inveterate isolationists, laggard and seemingly clubfooted in their foreign policies, because they still can't quite bring themselves to identify importantly with any experiences beyond their hemisphere. He suddenly understood that pang of glad exhilaration which briefly teared the eyes of a heroine in a Henry James story, an American girl long stranded in the elaborate intrigues of European aristocracy, when she glimpsed one afternoon an American naval vessel moored in a European port with American seamen casually gathered on the deck in their white summer uniforms, clean and crisp and chaste and remote, silent, like some momentary visitation of angels.

Boarding his flight to Amman, waiting for a moment with the Arab passengers at the bottom of the steps leading up into the plane, he found himself, when the door opened, in the midst of an unmanageable brawl of elbows and shoulders, a confusion of flourished passports, as if at any instant the whims of bureaucracy might conspire to cease accepting more passengers.

In the air on the way to Jordan, the plane turned south to skirt below the Sinai Peninsula, then tilted and swung East again with, at last, the mammoth flank of Africa—still as old and empty here as that memoryless time before the first emergence of man on grass veldts some thousand miles farther to the south—receding hugely, slowly under the wing. The plane now turned north, passing up the emptiness of the Arabian Peninsula, nearing Jordan—those high austere plains and slopes from which, three thousand years ago, Joshua's gaunt vagabond hosts contemplated at last Jericho and Canaan, the Promised Land.

II

On Jordan's Banks

On Jordan's stormy banks I stand,
    and cast a wishful eye
To Canaan's fair and happy land,
    where my possessions lie. . . .
    —First Lines of an Old Southern
    Protestant Hymn

Now, on the meager mountain road from the airport into Amman, the American passed through a countryside which had the oddly vacant and forsaken look of a no man's land—grassy Biblical hills with rubbled traces of tidy stone walls, high ridges ragged with rocks across which dandelions were blowing in a chill afternoon wind. There was only a solitary Bedouin tent here and there patched together with fluttering scraps, like a bat's wing, close to the flank of a hill, and an occasional herdsman or two following the long slow rippling of his goats down some steep nibbled slope. Entering Amman, he found it no more than a small mountain town constructed low to the hillside, with modest buildings of biscuit-colored stone under dwarfish evergreens. After the sweltering impactment of Egypt's cities, he felt curiously refreshed here; there seemed something immediately comfortable and reassuring about arriving in a small sovereignty, moving among authorities and enclosures and spaces designed on a more demure scale, tailored to an easier human reach.

But he soon became aware of a dark presence brooding everywhere around him—a ragged dislodged people who since 1948 had been encamped in this windblown country and who, after 1967, suddenly materialized as the new dynamic in the crisis: the Palestinians.

He had seen the first one, actually, as he was signing in at the Jordan Intercontinental Hotel—a youth with an undernourished gauntness strangely reminiscent of the portrait of Billy the Kid lounging in casual drowsy murderousness in that old faded daguerreotype—ambling across the polished pot-planted expanse of the lobby in the camouflage suit of the fedayeen with a bandoleer and Kalashnikov submachine gun slung over his shoulder, his head wrapped bandit-like in a *hatta*: a dark scorched figure who looked as if he had just wandered out of some violent inferno, but whose quiet incidental appearance in the lobby caused no more than a few mild glances from the waiters behind the glass wall of the bar. (Three months later, in the newsreel footage out of the Jordanian desert, he imagined he recognized that figure again ambling with the same offhand air of lethality around the beached and helpless hulks of three jetliners.)

Later that night he sat on a balcony overlooking a cramped back street with two Palestinians, both of whom had flourished respectably in Jordan, one of them a television newscaster and the other a professor of political science at Amman's university; after one pause, the newscaster—a woman—looked out over the terraced rooftops and said, "It is a beautiful city at this hour, with all its lights twinkling. But it is so full of misery—so full of quiet misery," and suddenly the professor lunged up, loomed over the American, a dim heavy shape with his arms lifted against the stars: "Yes, and I will tell you something, my friend. The Americans think we will just go away, we are of no real concern. Well, let the Americans think whatever they want and do whatever they want—it makes absolutely no difference to the situation. Because the Zionists, those murderers over there, will be gone someday. I promise you this, my dear fellow—if I fail, if my children fail, if my grandchildren fail, my *great*-grandchildren will drive them out of that land. . . ."

Being a Southerner, he was not unacquainted himself with the dark glamours of irreconcilability. His own land had long had a talent for it. He knew, for instance, of certain shabby little settlements in several wild corners of Brazil which were founded a century ago by expatriate Southern families who—out of simple raging refusal to accept machinations of history—fled the South with their slaves in the shambles right after Appomattox and undertook to preserve their ante-bellum culture on an alien continent. Now, after a hundred years, there remain in these settlements semblances of that old doomed order—shelves of Sir Walter Scott under the ancient flags and cavalry sabers, preaching and fried chicken every Sunday, even a slow languid drawl in speech. But over the years there were deviations in breeding, with both the descendants of the slaves and surrounding natives, and also—perhaps as a defense against that—among close relatives. The communities now for the most part have dwindled away into spidery old ladies and vague old men—prisoners, as it were, of their ancestors' indomitable intransigence—who are generally tended to and looked after by the others, the Negroes and half-breeds who have become the merchants and farmers of these communities. This same profound incapacity to accede, to grant less, had also endured in the land these original families had left, had continued to haunt it in the mien and embellishments of elegiac romance. In truth, he was no stranger to the mood. But what he discovered in Jordan—this full three months before the explosions of the hijacked airliners in the Jordanian desert, and at Cairo airport, the butcherous convulsions that followed in the plains and cities of Jordan—was an irreconcilability whose sheer integrity left him with permanent aversions to all romances of aggrievements. To be sure, the speculation was beginning to gather in the United States that, in 1948, the expiation and atonement for one monstrous two-thousand-year crime actually might have been purchased, quietly, at the price of another. Whatever, he found before him a people living a life which was itself the very metaphor, the image, of a mortal refusal to forget and to relinquish.

On the way back to his hotel after talking with the two Palestinians on the balcony, he happened to pass a camp on the outskirts of the city, this one dating back to 1948—a warren of mortar hovels still untouched by electricity after twenty years, a dingy murk of smoke along its dirt curbs from aftersupper trash fires, smoldering cardboard, and fruit peels. He heard once, from a dark corner they had just passed, a short metallic chatter like a brief sentence tacked out on a typewriter, and his driver quickly muttered without taking his eyes off the road, "Is nothing, nothing, don worry—they just shooting off their guns into the air a little bit, they are doing it all the time down here. Feel no alarm, is nothing to do with you. . . ."

Finally, on a blowing dusty afternoon, he was taken by Al Fatah—which has become in a sense the Establishment organ-

ization among the Palestinian commandos—to a refugee camp
a few miles outside Amman, he and his Fatah escort riding in
a panel truck driven by a glowering youth, wolfish and withdrawn with a neglected soot of beard on his cheeks, a submachine gun on the seat beside him as he savagely wheeled and
stomped and geared the truck on out of Amman into wide bat-
terings of wind hauling out of the bright immense empty spaces
of the afternoon, past scrawls of barbed wire spattered with the
scraps of paper skidding and pinwheeling across the road, past
the plodding figures of old women swathed in tautly rippling
black cloth. Presently he saw before him an entire valley littered
with tents and tin sheds no larger than chicken coops, numberless into the distance, with a Palestinian flag—one single daub
of color—flickering from a hut on a hill. Stopping at this hut,
they got out of the truck into white gales of dust, and proceeded
down a slope into the camp, past grassless dirt lanes where children in white rubber rain boots were playing with tufts of weeds
in motor-oil cans, and a few women—some of them heavily
pregnant—were trudging to the water drums wrapped like
mummies against the dust that came in crazy scurries around
corners. Washing lashed and plunged from stringlines, and there
was the sound here and there of a baby's thin inextinguishable
crying under the mindless slapping of a tent side while tinny
music dreamed faintly from a radio playing somewhere in waning antique sunlight. It somehow evoked an Okie shantytown
from that wild-eyed time of dust storms between America's two
world wars. Most of the people in this camp, his escort informed
him, had been country people, small farmers suddenly translated from their fields and pastures on the other side of the Jordan into this congested shadeless kennel of rags and tin sheeting,
and he noticed beside some of the shacks small plots of onions

and tomatoes—his guide, nodding toward them, smiled. "You see? They still try to remember the land. . . ."

They reached at last a cement hut on top of a hill at the other side of the camp—a single bleak room with wooden benches against the mortared walls—where he found five Palestinian men sitting quietly in a circle just inside the door, their weathered faces swathed in *hattas,* squinting through thin ribbonings of smoke from the cigarettes in their lumpish heavy hands. On the floor behind them, a youth was sitting on a blanket tenderly cleaning the disassembled parts of a Kalashnikov with rags and kerosene from a Molotov cocktail. One of them—an older man who was gripping a whittled walking stick with both hands between his knees—told the American, "I myself, I had in Jericho a small shop, a coffeehouse. When the fighting is starting in '67, I leave, come to Jordan. Then, after some many months, I go back to my house in Jericho and I am captured and put in prison by the Israelis. 'Why did you come back from Amman,' they ask me, and I say, 'What do you mean? This is my home. Why I should not come back to my home?' So they say, 'No, this is not your home now. This all belong to Israel.' They keep me in prison for three, four month, until I go on hunger strike, you know. So they release me. They take me to the bridge, and when I get out, you know, start across, they *kick* me—yes, with boot, kick me, and say, 'Stay, now. Never come back across again.' " He released one hand from the walking stick to gesture, and his palm was damp with sweat: "You ask, I tell you —the hostilities we feel now, they cannot be described. Look out there, what you see. What did the Palestinians do to merit this punishment? What crime did we commit to be treated like this?"

There was a silence. Outside in the bleak flare of the afternoon, the wind was still barging dustily, buffeting against the boarded windows of the room. One man sitting beside the doorway—his legs crossed and tightly entwined, a fatigue cap wadded in one bony hand—abruptly swung his long houndlike face toward the American: "If the American people believe the Palestinians are not politically educated now, they are making a mistake. We have to know everything in the world—the radios, the loud-speakers in the camp, they even tell us of the speeches in the American Congress. We know America is using Israel as a base for the protecting of the American interests, we realize the real enemy of the Arab people is America. This is made clear to us every day when we see the American tanks and Phantoms hitting our people, killing our children. We know that without the help of America, we would not be in this camp now, none of this would have happened to us. We would still be back in our lands and our homes. So now every difficulty of our life, each day here, reminds us of America. The bad weather comes, that is America. Wind blows the dust in our faces, that is America. We are cold in the winter, there is mud everywhere, our chil- dren cry around us—we think again upon America. All this"— he flourished his clenched cap toward the door—"America. No, we do not forget America. We remember her every day. . . ."

After the American had returned to the States, it seemed to him the land had been full of forebodings of what erupted there three months later—those uncanny five days of abandoned slaughter between the Palestinians and Hussein's troops. The American went with the Fatah guide to another camp, climbing up a stony rise scattered with can lids and chicken feathers to a long shed of corrugated tin and raw plank rafters, a kind of makeshift tabernacle, where a political revival meeting was under way. A ragged crowd was gathered outside in the bare yard in the stark sunshine, listening to a high thin strumming voice which, he saw when he finally managed to get a glimpse inside, came from a reedy youth standing tense and rigid in a sweltering room that was filled with shawled men sitting cross-legged on the floor: "Before 1967, we were waiting for others to deliver us. But now we know we must deliver ourselves. We have taken it into our own hands. The way of Islam says never rely on others for your own hopes. The way of Islam is self-dependence. For we must separate between the Western and the Eastern Arab countries. Since the Zionists, the Arab people have always been divided. The Western world has continuously worked against the people of Muh-hammm-mut"—the name was uttered in a long broken moan—"but it was in Muh-hammm-mut that the Arab peoples created a great empire! We were masters then, while now we are slaves and servants. But, brethren, we are still the children of Muh-hammm-mut! The way is clear. It is armed struggle for the liberation of our Palestine. The time is coming, brethren. The time is near. . . ." As the voice rang on like the dronings of a tuning fork in the hot afternoon, the American—standing outside with the crowd in a hum of flies writing in the damp pages of his notebook while his guide translated in a low mumble—gradually began to feel again those dull intimations in his lower belly with which he had been skirmishing ever since Egypt; leaning against the rippled-tin side of the shed, he became aware he was covered with a chill film of sweat. He looked up then into the stares of the men in the yard. *My God,* he thought, *do I look that strange? Could it be I'm about to faint?* Stuffing his notebook back in his hip pocket, he motioned to his guide, and they walked back down the hill to the car. Tumbling into the back seat and clapping the door shut and then leaning back, he realized he was panting, his heart hammering with a furious lightness. *What the hell,* he thought, *I just need to eat something, a good full meal.* As they drove away, the voice from the shed at the top of the hill rang brightly on in the afternoon, toneless, ecstatic, fading and faint, and then gone.

"Let us say you have been living in a house," a Fatah officer told him several days later, "and you decide to allow this family which has no place to stay to live in one of your rooms. Soon you discover they have moved in more members of their family, they have taken over two more of your rooms. All of a sudden, you find it has been arranged, by powerful parties outside your neighborhood, that they will take over your entire house, and so you are evicted and simply told to find a place elsewhere; you must board with your neighbors so this family can have your house. Afterward, people come by the house and say, 'Why, look how beautiful the lawn is kept,' and they go inside and tell each other, 'Why, look at these lovely paintings on the wall—what a pleasant place they have made of this house.' But what they forget is that the gardens and the paintings are not the central issue about this house. The central and relevant issue is: whose house is it?"

Actually, in this dispute over the legitimate tenants of Palestine, it is frequently maintained, not only by Israelis but by other political academicians, that there are no true native Palestinian folk, that most Palestinians are in fact descended from fathers and grandfathers who arrived in the land around the turn of the century when the first tentative Zionist settlements began to be answered by deliberate countermigrations from Syria, Iraq, Lebanon. But trying to trace any single thread of legitimacy back through the labyrinths of this region's chronology, trying to construct any geopolitical morality through the perspective of history here, is like gazing down an interminable hall of mirrors; even those days in 1948 of Israel's annunciation and the flight of the Palestinians amount, finally, to a blind welter of mutual provocation and intimidation, terror and outrage and retaliation, in which morality becomes finally mute.

For any proper historical answer, one would have to grope on back through the centuries, all the way to the ultimate question: where are the Canaanites? Across the slopes and plains of this worn and oldest earth, ever since Sumer and Abraham, warfares and momentary imperial grandeurs have passed like a ceaseless gusting of locusts; the first guttering candles of history—mosaics excavated from the royal cemeteries of Ur, the 4,300-year-old stele of Naram-Sim, king of Akkad—reveal men already engaged here in a fitful grappling for each other's lands; Amalekites, Amerites, Hittites, Assyrians, Babylonians, Philistines, Persians blundering endlessly after each other with periodic expeditions by Egypt, empires trampling back and forth in a compulsive bloody enterprise of appropriation and dispossession that was undistracted by any U.N. resolution, any global attentiveness and conscience, any restraints or constrictions exerted by the abstract interests of two remote massive powers. (Something endearingly innocent, something touchingly hopeful and dauntless, some provincial joy and affection, he silently celebrated as he listened one evening to an American professor—a gangling crane-like figure with a boyish sun-pinked face—sedulously resolving the whole difficulty of Palestine with a glad wholesome earnestness: constructing in a hotel-roof restaurant, high over Jordan's ancient earth of numberless unremembered battles, a sensible sturdy plain edifice of rationality with a Midwestern architecture of decency and good will.)

But however dubious the historical certification, in effect Palestine does exist now. An Israeli intellectual was to muse some weeks later in Tel Aviv, "It's quite likely, of course, that we ourselves—beginning with 1948, then in 1956, but finally with 1967—we ourselves, Israel, created them authentically as a nation." One Jordanian government minister acknowledged, "It's always been considered, all over the Arab world, that no one is more like the Jews than the Palestinians—certainly, of all Arabs, they're closest to the Jews in terms of business enterprise, ambition for their children, competitiveness. It may be simply because they have lived in such close conjunction with them. But the feeling of many Arabs has been that the Palestinians are more like the Jews than they are the Arabs; they are even called sometimes the Arab Jews."

For Israel, probably the gravest complication of the 1967 victory was the new implacability it produced among the Palestinians. A Palestinian girl married to a Jordanian doctor studying in Atlanta told the American there one afternoon before he left, "Those days before the June War, you know, we would hear on the radio about the Arab armies massing; it was the maximum showdown and everything would be over within only a few days. I was a student then in Lebanon," she reminisced in a rustling voice, a delicate and demure smile on her face, "and after classes, my friends and I would gather around a radio listening to the announcements, and we would tell each other, 'Poor Israel. What are we going to be able to do for them afterward? How will we take care of them all?' That's true—for all our lives we'd never really had the feeling of belonging anywhere, but now when it seemed for the first time ever we were actually close, finally so close to returning to our land, to having a home again, all we talked about was how we would care for the Jews, making all these plans about taking in different Jewish families. I remember we felt so *sorry* for them, listening to the radio in our rooms those afternoons—one girl even began crying once. And even the second day of the war, the third day, we still had no idea. Then suddenly Israel was on the Suez Canal, Nasser was resigning. . . . After that, forever since, you know, there has been a different feeling. I mean just no one cares what happens to them any more, whatever it may have to be, whether they are all driven into the sea or not. It is a bad thing, I know, to feel this way, but we can't help it."

The war of 1967—that astonishing victory of Israel's which has seemed ever since to be slowly turning inside out for her—also left a new mood in the Arab countries. One Egyptian official confessed, "A very unhealthy thing, as I view it, has begun to develop since 1967. It may surprise you that there was ever a disposition toward any sympathy or generosity for Israel anywhere in Egypt, but you must believe me that one found it before 1967; it was always quietly there beneath the speeches, and it was a fact that always seemed to me to offer some hope. After all, we had been dwelling together in this part of the world for a very long time, there were never the kind of pogroms and persecutions here that occurred in Russia and the West, and if you talked to some chap on the street, he would tell you, 'But they are our brothers, we are all the children of Abraham. Why should they want to do hurt to us?' But since 1967 this has completely disappeared. There is nothing now but outright hatred and bitterness, which is certainly not good for Israel, but even more, not good for us."

As one native Palestinian who left a European university faculty to join Al Fatah after the Six-Day War explained, "For twenty years, you see, we were divided all over the Arab world, separated from each other, the Palestinians in the Gaza Strip kept secluded by Egypt and told to wait, just to wait, listen to your radio and we will tell you when the time comes. So we stayed fragmented, glued to Radio Cairo, Radio Damascus, Radio Baghdad—these were the days of the transistor struggle, the transistor dispersal. We kept expecting change to come as some explosive, cataclysmic event—sudden and complete, achieved by others. So we kept listening to our radios for it to happen. Then, of course, 1967 destroyed the myth—the myth of success through classical armies, but most importantly the myth of an outside deliverance. For various reasons, of course, the Arab governments still desired to keep their fingers in the pie, so to speak, but we recognized the revolution had to be independent of them, that we had to take up armed struggle without waiting to be able to match Israeli technology, and that it would have to be a long, slow, patient struggle—indeed, that we could not separate this struggle from central reference points and identifications in other struggles outside the Arab world. This is what 1967 accomplished. And I will tell you that now, beyond the possibility of annihilating us altogether, the question of any external control from the Arab governments does not exist."

But as a political fact, Palestine still remains in a kind of violent abeyance, diffused thinly through Israel, more thickly and indigestibly in the occupied territories like Gaza, but most conspicuously in Jordan in the form of a bewildering array of military and political cadres—an uncertainly emerging nation within another nation which is itself a kind of arbitrary invention, a relic of the Balkanization of the Middle East after World War I with a name that could have been lifted out of some Biblical fairy tale: the Hashemite Kingdom of Jordan. More or less a political abstraction scantily populated by nomads and ruled over by a royal house from Saudi Arabia, there is still a certain spiffy British look to its bantam military, and to its present Sandhurst-educated sovereign, King Hussein (one Israeli later said with a sniff, "Such a proper little Englishman, he is"), a tidy diminutive figure, precise and excruciatingly polite, with meltingly amiable eyes and a thin slight boyish neck which gives him a peculiarly vulnerable look. As if Hussein were compensating for the political dubiousness of his state, the American found everywhere in Amman official portraits of him smiling hospitably and hopefully in an endless variety of royal and military uniforms—a gallery of photographs showing him with his fabled Legion, firing a pistol and gamely clambering aboard tanks—until finally the American got the impression that Hussein's principal exercise of authority consisted of posing for official pictures. But there seemed about this sovereign something of the uneasy air of a captive host—a decent doughty beleaguered little prince who as a boy saw his grandfather, a moderate and placable realist regarding Israel, assassinated by a Palestinian as the two of them were praying in a mosque, and who was living now in the uncertainty of whether his kingdom existed only at the sufferance of these same refugees it was harboring. Indeed, the American moved in Jordan through indefinite cross-eddyings of separate authorities: both Palestinian and Royal Jordanian roadblocks, dual clearances from both government ministries and guerrilla offices. In effect, the camps were sovereignties unto themselves, Palestinian vehicles even bearing their own license tags. The result was a sense in Jordan of some curious and uneasy political irresolution, a lack of any final political validity and substance, unlike the monolithic management one feels in Egypt. The American came across what seemed odd lapses of concentration: one evening in the restaurant atop the

Jordan Intercontinental, he paused with his fork in midair, startled, as he heard the dinner-hour combo begin the theme from *Exodus,* and a few moments later he paused again, incredulous, as they began playing a Jewish wedding march.

"The truth is," one Jordanian professor declared, "there is no government in this country." And in this limbo of authority, the American found himself in the midst of a general casual flourishing of weapons along sidewalks, at hotel luncheon counters, in cabs, that gave Amman rather the look of some Western frontier town like Tombstone, Arizona, or Virginia City before the arrival of marshals and judges. After a while, he realized he was growing accustomed to their simple proximity —his elbow bumping a submachine-gun barrel, a muzzle pointing from the front seat of a car directly at the pack of Trues in his shirt pocket, no longer quite distracted him as at first.

Finally, though, the Palestinians seemed to be the orphans of the Arab world, suspended not only in an alienation inside Jordan, but in a certain estrangement from the whole Arab community and ethos. "I would have to say," remarked one Palestinian leader, "that the celebrated classic Arab intoxication with God simply isn't relevant to this new generation of Palestinians. This struggle could never become a holy war for them —it's larger than that." Even while they had created considerable popular excitement in the Arab countries, they remained essentially isolated from the governments of many of those countries. "I would remind you of something Farouk said once," the Palestinian professor proposed that evening on the balcony overlooking Amman. "He told a group of his friends not long after Nasser overthrew him that the very near future would find only five kings left in the world—the King of England, and the kings

83

of hearts, clubs, spades, and diamonds. The U.S. thinks it can depend on its satraps in the Arab world to constrain us—Saud and Bourguiba and this—this tin puppet we have here. But they will be gone soon. Every one of them."

Indeed, with the Palestinian intellectuals—the doctors, attorneys, professors—who suddenly materialized from far points after the 1967 war to give the movement a political articulation, it seemed to aspire more to some new Algeria or Spain, but with the special complication of having to operate by a remote control outside the land. Lacking this elementary physical backdrop, it suggested a labor something like an abstract play with actors alone feverishly conjuring life out of a spotlit emptiness surrounded by darkness. Actually, the reality of Palestine now, it was maintained, is an existential one: it is an existential nation. "True revolutions begin, you see, as a common communion of experience among a people," asserted one Palestinian spokesman. "It is true that the habit, the tendency, still lingers to mistake pronouncements for deeds—and I will have to confess that some of our organizations still seem to invest a lot more energy in propaganda than operations. But we know we must keep words and deeds close together. Rather than cant, we are developing our ideology and our structure out of the continuing experience of this struggle, which has to do with the rather basic and primitive problem of not being able to live in your own home and till your own fields—the simple aim is liberation, and armed struggle is its means. It is not out of dogma or theory that we are acting. Whatever dogma or theory or political philosophy finally shapes the Palestinian state will arise out of our actions, our experience in achieving that state. You cannot necessarily understand your immediate reality, much less change it, by reading translations from Chairman Mao. A party, of course, will tend to seek ideological justification later on just to perpetuate itself, but a revolutionary is one who makes a revolution, not one who talks about it."

When he visited in Amman the disparate rented basement crannies and outlying huts from which this fugitive revolution was being directed, which were as yet the only physicality of the Palestinian state—bare tile-floored cubicles teeming constantly with booted guerrillas in dappled suits, naked light bulbs dangling from cords over battered metal desks and filing cabinets, metal crates of ammunition shoved in corners, submachine guns lying on tabletops beside pocket radios—it seemed to the American that he did, indeed, catch ghosts of Spain in the thirties. He usually found an eclectic assortment of fringe figures haunting these places: a perpetual clump of sleepless journalists roosting in the front yards, a marginalia of lounging cabdrivers and anonymous young females, as well as such occasional curiosities as a peripatetic American Jew who had been an anti-Zionist pamphleteer ever since 1948.

Then, at the end of one day of talks with another fedayeen command, the American, rising to return to his hotel, was told by his driver, "Outside on the porch, I think, there are some American volunteers. I told them that you were here." As he left, he passed them in the dusk—four lank youths gathered off at one end of the porch, unkempt and dusty and looking a bit haggard and displaced—and he exchanged with them only a quick furtive glance, a fleeting nod acknowledging the embarrassment and guilt they appeared to share as journalist and partisans involved in a deadly foreign imbroglio.

He asked a Fatah spokesman one evening if, in the end, his vision of "a liberated homeland with a democratic Palestinian society where all will live in equal participation" did not mean the inevitability of an awesome amount of blood. He was answered by an expression of mild wistfulness. The official had been a professor of political science in London who had taken the name of Abu Omar when he joined Fatah—a thirtyish young man with a certain clean-shaven and antiseptic look, horn-rim glasses and fine-spun hair, and a precisioned manner: "Yes, of course, there will have to be a great deal of blood—very much blood, I'm afraid. But you must understand, it's not as though we have suddenly impatiently resorted to armed struggle. We waited for twenty years, you know. It's just that there is simply nothing left for it now but blood." He seemed to maintain a vegetarian's air of relentless abstemiousness, pleasantly declining another journalist's invitation for a drink with a slight smile. "If you wish to talk further about these matters—but for just a social chat, excuse me, I do thank you, but I'm afraid we aren't able to take out time for such things. . . ." The American asked Omar if the fedayeen's absorption in the brutal business of transacting a Palestinian state would not leave them unfit in some deep irreparable way to preside eventually over the business of a nation's rich full life in peace. Omar shrugged: "Perhaps. Yes, that could be—maybe, for that time, when it comes, there will have to be other leaders. But it is a matter we cannot think about now." Asked about his own life before 1967, Omar smiled wistfully. "My personal life is not important. One has no private life now, no private self. It is a price you have to pay. You subdue the individual to the common struggle, and what you find is that, in giving yourself to the common struggle, you actually enhance yourself, you are enlarged, you are in fact reborn. Is there not a passage in your New Testament?—'Whosoever would save his life shall lose it, but whosoever will lose his life for my sake, shall find it.' That is the way it is with all of us."

Indeed, it seemed they all had consigned themselves to a scrupulously cultivated anonymity in which their only assumption of identity again—their only resurrection—lay in death. "In our movement now," one fedayeen spokesman told the American in a tense and almost worshipful murmur, "the only men who are photographed, the only ones who are spoken about, are the dead ones: the martyrs." He pronounced the word like a soft fondling, "mar-tears." The American sensed they were all involved in some high romance of death, dwelling dreamily in the perpetual impending of that final exalting event. While he was talking with another Fatah official one afternoon, a youth suddenly entered the room—a tall ramshackle figure, with a tangled tuft of black hair, his sport shirt drooping loosely over baggy trousers, grinning a little sheepishly—and the Fatah official lunged up and embraced him, kissed him elaborately on both cheeks, and then explained to the American, with the youth sitting beside him, "This is one who was on the Lebanese border when the Israelis made their raid. We did not hear from him for days; everyone thought he was a casualty," and he turned to the youth again—who was still grinning, returned touched with a brief glamour from that ultimate dark sanctification—and clapped him on the back.

Finally, the American suspected it was a mystique which actually provided the only meaning for their lives: having existed pointlessly and unassimilated in their camps for twenty years, at the least it was something—motion, passion, exertion, however desperate—to live for. In one bare little room, he talked with a group of "militia girls" who had been assembled for him by his Fatah guide—all of them teen-agers engaged in guerrilla training who had not seen their parents since 1967, arranged now in a circle of chairs before him like a collection of Campfire

Girls, a bit fluttery at first in their heavy soldiers' uniforms, their faces fresh and bright with, already, the darkly eloquent eyes of Arab women. One profession of faith, gravely offered by a somewhat hefty and grim-lipped girl, was, as it turned out in translation, rather less than political: "I found in the movement the opportunity to get rid of the tensions I lived in, for I was raised in very conservative circumstances. My parents would not even let me go out of the house. Now the movement has become the first step to a new and wider life." But as they continued explaining their commitments, with a unanimous manner of un-remitting tremulous earnestness, the session began to assume something of the quality of a Pentecostal youth-revival testi-monial meeting—"You need a militia to protect the people from counterrevolutionists, and also, after the experience of the June War with no militia on the West Bank, it was clear that if we had been given weapons the Zionists would not have come in as easily as they did. Chairman Mao Tse-tung has said that it is not a shame for you to let the enemy into your land; the shame is if you let him out. . . ." Each of their declarations was inter-preted by the Fatah guide at his elbow, in a quiet monotone as if he were not so much translating their messages as secretly describing them: "She says that she differentiates between her friends and her enemies by the weapons that are used against her people, that she saw her three brothers killed by napalm from Phantoms. The Zionists use the American weapons while her people use the Socialist weapons, and her right and her hope of her home is like the sun: it rises in the east," while they leaned toward him with a flushing urgency under the damp boiled glare of the light bulb, vibrant, their faces almost imploring, but re-moved that one lapsed gap of the translation beyond him, their thin intent voices uttering unintelligible sounds, sibilants, warblings. "She says that all her life has been spent in a camp, that dated from 1948, and the Arabs would always say, 'Look at those refugees, how they are living,' so that her dignity and self-respect were damaged; she faced always many questions about herself. When she was a child, there was no one to take care of her, no one to direct her, and her life was without purpose. But now with the movement there have come those who can direct her life and emotions, and expand her knowledge. She has found her place. The old generation was confused, but the new generation knows the way is paved now; all things are new for them and they are organized. The change is not so much in more personal freedoms, but in a guidance and commitment to the revolution, so that she is growing up knowing her role and her place; she is feeling the same now with the Vietnamese, the Black Panthers and Che Guevara and Mao Tse-tung, who led China from a very lazy people to a very active people."

One thin and wispy child who seemed to huddle shyly inside the bulky wrappings of her guerrilla gear, her small feet just brushing the floor, spoke to the Fatah translator in a barely audible voice. "She is waiting for the chance now to give herself completely to the revolution as a full commando, so that she may actively fight. It is all she is living for now, for that time. Her heroes, the people she believes in, are the mar-tears of our struggle." The American gazed, vaguely incredulous, at their softly blooming faces as the translator muttered on at his elbow, ". . . She wants to be like those mar-tears who have exploded themselves with enemy tanks, those who can overcome anything and who put barbed wire around themselves"—and suddenly he realized they were all like young nuns, novices, plucked in the first unconscious luster of life into a fierce and amorous piety, ethereality, a discipline whose dry irrelevancies were all their entranced tongues knew: only, they were not unravished brides of God; they were in love with death. . . . "She says she most admires the Arabic woman who once lost three sons in battle, and who received the news of their deaths not with sadness and despair but with happiness and rejoicing, as if she had received news of their weddings. . . ."

The American spent one morning at a school on the outskirts of Amman which is maintained by Fatah for the daughters of all commandos slain in operations against Israel and which is managed by a brisk pleasant dumpling of a woman with hair drawn wispily back in a bun. She explained, "We have now seventy-eight girls, from all the organizations. There are even ten girls here from Syria. After a fighter is killed in battle, right away we visit his family. At first, of course, some of them cannot accept giving up their girls to the revolution; they think it means they will lose them forever, but we explain to them that families visit them twice a month, and they are allowed to spend three weeks together every summer in the camps." Strolling along the school's stark cool corridors, with scrubbed linoleum floors and chill radiators set against blank gray walls, she continued, "We have schoolwork from seven-thirty in the morning until one in the afternoon, with exercises and military drills after lunch. Three times a week there are Hebrew lessons. We must know their language for the future. We are in need of a strong new generation to accomplish the liberation of Palestine, and we are preparing them for that long effort, and for the return home."

In the prefab school sheds outside, he found an English classroom whose play-board walls were decorated with laboriously executed posters bearing slogans like "Revolution Until Victory!" along with pictures scissored from American fashion magazines: one sentence, "This is Mummy," illustrated by what looked like a Clairol Shampoo ad, a preened blond creature with commercial prettiness, laughing and swinging her hair like a luminous American angel in a golden ambience; "I am a Man" illustrated by a bronzed skier in a bright Christmas-red sweater leaning forward with a brilliant grin in the crystal sunshine of some enemy Alpine slope. Showing the modest rooms of the dormitory building, with scatterings of dolls over simple bunks fashioned from gray pipe and with military uniforms hanging alongside small frocks in the closets, the headmistress pointed out, "We call all the rooms after cities and towns in Palestine, you notice. We keep them always in touch with the revolution —we remind them, 'What town, once again, did your family come from in Palestine? And your father—in what battle, now, did he die?' We tell them that our people were living in Palestine in peace with the Jews; we were all friends until the Zionists began coming to establish a state which would spread from the Euphrates to the Nile, and the British and other imperialist countries helped them do this. It is very hard for them, of course, to remember the difference between the Jews and the Zionists," and she paused now in the hall to note, "It seems hard for children to understand distinctions. My own daughter was only two years old when the June War broke out in 1967—we were living in Nablus, which was then in Jordan, and with all the shooting and exploding, the bombs, she was clinging to me all the time; she never wanted to leave the house, and whenever we had to go into the streets she wanted me to hold her all the time; she would keep her face buried in my shoulder everywhere we went, until we were back in our house again. Then we came to Jordan, and the first time she saw some Jordanian soldiers on the street, she came running to me crying. I tried to tell her, 'No, no—these are Arabs, these are our people, you must not be afraid of them,' but she couldn't be comforted—'They are the same ones we saw in Nablus,' she kept saying. 'They are the same ones. They are here, too. . . .' "

He lingered in the doorway of one room where, on a lower bunk by an open window, he saw the slight nestled form of a small girl sleeping—a child not more than a toddler, fashioned, it seemed, out of an old Victorian sentimentality, with Botticellian curls which damply filigreed cheeks touched with the palest stain of strawberry, wisps of hair brushed back from one fragile ear, a light blanket pulled up around her shoulders, and one small plump hand curled with a soft delicacy beside her slightly parted lips. "Her father was killed in the June War, before she was born," the headmistress whispered. "There was no one to look after her, so we took her in. Her mother remarried, someone in the camp here, a difficult man who did not like having this child of the other man with them—a very sad, very unfortunate situation." Outside the open window by her bed, from the courtyard between the corrugated-tin classrooms, there was the quiet steady thumping of a volleyball, a light glittering of voices in the morning, where the older girls were playing in gray pinstriped jumpers around a flower bed of yellow daisies and petunias, with a small flagpole in the center from which there slowly coiled a Palestinian flag. Then, abruptly, someone began clanging a handbell, and the soft bright sounds of their play ceased in the morning air; there was a brief scuffling as they collected themselves in the gravel yard into the precise stenciled pattern of military ranks under the imperious brisk clang of the bell—but with that sudden brazen summons, the child on the bed stirred only briefly, vaguely, as if the morning breeze passing through the window over her cuddled still form had carried to her some dim uneasy fleeting dream, the rumor of some far furious telling reaching down through the deep leagues of her quiet and perfect sleep.

Shortly before he left Jordan—on the anniversary of Israel's official inauguration as a state, twenty-two years since those ensuing convulsions which had left the Palestinians littered as refugees along the shores of surrounding Arab countries—they gathered early in the morning out of the camps and training bases, into a long steep street of Amman for a march down to the ancient Greco-Roman amphitheatre in the center of the city where a rally was to be held. Multiple loudspeakers were blaring, white banners bobbing over an infinite glinting thicket of weapons. When at last they began moving down the street, it was like the slow terrific slippage of a landslide, with a sudden issue of huge shouts up and down the formations, the street filled now with multitudinous clapping, chants like many deep-chambered Gregorian laments. The American was accompanied this morning by another Fatah functionary, a somewhat famished-looking youth with a dull yellow pallor like a nicotine stain and wet black eyes, wearing a limply hung black sharkskin suit, his black mop of hair sodden in the heat. "They are saying their home is the gun," he reported with a grin, "only living in their guns can they restore themselves. They are saying, 'Our unity is through blood, we offer ourselves to the martyrs. . . .' " They moved massively and sluggishly on down the hill, passing with a blattering of motorcycles beneath balconies and rooftops brimming with applauding people—formations of Lion Cubs, copper-hued boys in guerrilla uniforms, stamping fiercely with arms rigidly lashing, the front ranks bearing floral wreaths behind crawling jeeps prickly with submachine guns, trucks in which there were crouched female commandos, their faces masked in wound *hattas*. "This is our last chance, you see," his

Fatah guide told him as they were waiting to cross at one corner. "We have already had three chances—in 1948, '56, and
'67. If we lose this chance, there will never be another one. This
time, we either win or we will keep going until there is nothing
for them, either; it will all be destroyed." The American
thought that he detected something abandoned and berserk loose
now in the morning (a sensation he recalled later back in the
States when he first heard of the plane hijackings and the hysterias that had been loosed over that land). Stepping down from
the corner into the currents of the crowd, he became aware that
the Fatah guide was groping for his hand—no doubt a simple
unconscious solicitude—but he instantly, in some unaccountable
contraction of dread, snatched his hand away from the touch.

At last the procession reached the amphitheatre, entering it
like a sudden rapid-spreading suffusion of inky shadows across
the blind bone-white stones in the sunlight—a lost begrimed
dark-burnt army abruptly arrived out of some holocaust under a
violent swimming of flags, milling with faces muffled in *hattas,*
over the stumps of ruined columns, pedestals still dimly fluted
and scrolled from that vanished age of forgotten poetries, pipings, graces: the tragedies—Aeschylus, Sophocles, Euripides,
Seneca—which were once enacted here as formal ceremonies
translating the old chaotic furies of man's condition into a religious lyric music, until, when the Greek morning and Roman
noontide of that age came to its final enormous twilight, all that
was left of those original sacramental tragedies was the simple
savagery again, the ruthless elemental furies. And now, as if in
their rage and anguish drawn by some dim instinct, some unarticulated memory, back to this old site where those ancients
gathered for sanctifying observances of grief and fury and death,
they continued swarming in as loudspeakers rang electronically

94

over the stones, spreading up over the canyon of graven tiered
seats that rose at a dizzy tilt up to a high ridge scribbled with
barbed wire against a fierce blue enameled sky, a crest prowled
now by the dark noiseless figures of guerrilla sentries in vigilant
custodial appropriation of this old theatre, this temple for their
own ceremonies of vengeance. *But maybe the gods have just
changed now,* he thought; *maybe the engines of history and
revolution have become the fates. . . .*

The American suddenly found himself on the stage of the
theatre, moving through a tumult of bearded fedayeen chief-
tains, and then he realized the Palestinian guide had finally
fastened onto his hand: startled, it seemed to him for an
astonished moment that he was totally captured in that half-
accidental clasp, a grip like some sudden chill claim, the beginning of some final assimilation; discreetly, gently, he tried
to tug away, and finally with a quick wrench freed himself. The
Palestinian glanced back at him with a brief half smile of
puzzlement, and then merely motioned him on with a curt nod
of his head. . . .

But whatever impulse had brought them all here for this occasion did not hold—in fact, seemed to falter and flicker away,
as soon as they had arrived, into a fitful pointless anger, vicious
dogfights breaking out among them as the seats almost immediately began emptying again. Then, over the grounds outside the amphitheatre, they continued plunging back and forth
in aimless last surges of passion, through a haze of dust, with
finally a few tatters of machine-gun fire in the air. They gradually scattered away, the dust thinned and vanished behind them,
and the amphitheatre was left hushed and forsaken again in
the sunlight.

But when he got back to his hotel room, it seemed to him

he still felt on his hand a faint residue from the Palestinian's grasp. He spent several minutes at his bathroom sink scrubbing his hands with soap under the water from the faucet.

He was to be carried the next morning—his last day in Jordan —to a fedayeen post in the north for a guerrilla operation on the other side of the river, and that night as he sat in his hotel room it finally came to him that he might possibly be killed. It was the first time, actually, the notion had ever seriously entered his head. With some fascination now, he elaborately explored this prospect, and then, with mild disbelief, he realized he actually, incredibly, had begun to take notes on this intimate uneasiness—he stared at the careful tidy transcription in his notebook: "the triviality of all flesh . . ." and with a strange deep shiver he pitched notebook and pen across the room, into a far corner. *Wait a minute now,* he thought, *just what's going on here?* and was rapidly brought to a somewhat elemental pondering: namely, *What the hell am I really doing here, all of a sudden just six hours away from leaving for a Palestinian commando raid? There's no need to do this thing. . . .* It was not even, this time, the personal investment of urgent escape, self-melodrama, that, back when he was seventeen, his un-realized aborted adventure of joining Castro's mountain ir-regulars would have been. Now, thirteen years later, he was about to enter at least an approximation of that lost experience, but this time it was as a journalist, and with a detachment—a kind of amorality—that curiously seemed to make the danger, the possibility of death, somehow all the more palpable. In truth, it occurred to him that he was probably indulging in absurdly ponderous alarms: in all likelihood, the day would pass as innocuous. But the day was not here yet, indeed seemed years distant, and he was slung now in a suspension of time-less night anarchic with probabilities in which anything could happen, thinking, *Maybe this is even when the day itself is decided; maybe each day's small destinies are conceived and fashioned in the chaos of night out of which it is born,* thinking, *Damn, is it worth it now? I've got to decide now if this thing is really worth it* . . . even while the dismal queasiness, the sus-picion, began to gather that he had spent his life for so long in gestures, poses, imagination, artifice, abstract glamours, and moralities that he didn't know—he couldn't tell. He found himself, as it were, delivered into a crisis of abstractions and conceits, largely made up, he suspected, of Hemingway, Camus, Wolfe, the Gospels of Matthew, Mark, Luke, and John, not to mention Faulkner. His distress now was that—having posed the whole business as a matter of courage, a willingness to experience, even of the truth of his writing—he had actually contrived a lethal trap of abstractions. Peculiarly enough, he discovered himself groping back through it all for the old sturdy anchoring definitions in the Scriptures, holding on for a moment to a passage from Jeremiah: "The heart of men is deceitful above all things . . . who can know it?" Profoundly, he did not want to go. He wanted to be home. But he gradually realized—with the lamp burning in the room with that haloed glare of three o'clock in the morning—that he was captured in that trap of abstractions anyway. Because however artificial and histrionic and vain the demand for this extension seemed in the desperate rationality of this hour, he also knew that in the hallucinations of his spirit again in the weeks that followed, he would not be able to bear not having done it, could not afford now not to go—perhaps for the same reason that, engaged in that boyhood play called Making Leaps, crouched on one tree limb to jump to another, he would always finally sling himself on across that intervening space of emptiness which he had been contemplating for long breathless moments with dusty mouth, walloping heart, and an exquisite revulsion (indeed, as later on in the next day, he would actually be blindly insisting to the young fedayeen leader that they drive on to the river even though Israeli planes were bombing the road). But now as he sat in the close unblinking glare of his lamp, with its thin light hum of burning electricity filling the hushed room, sipping of the warm Scotch splashed into an iceless un-cellophaned hotel glass with a feeling of being filmed in some dingy moisture like the glistening gauze of a snail's passage—still not knowing why he was here and even who he was to have arrived at this unexpected intersection of life and death—he found he was simply yearning for the first dim shadowing of gray light in the closed curtains of his balcony doors, for the plain dull peaceful certainty of day, when it would be beyond him at last; the calm inevitable machinery of circumstances would begin and it might actually turn out that, having committed himself, he would not have to go after all; they would say it was all off; he might actually be back here in his room in just a few hours getting into bed to finally sleep, deeply, completely, dreamlessly.

But at seven o'clock, when he left his room and started down the hall, one of the Palestinian room attendants waiting by the elevator door grinned and gave him a light startling wink, like a signal announcing an irrevocable judgment: "You go to Irbid today, eh? Be with the commandos? . . ."

His driver, Abdullah, was waiting for him in the lobby—a small crisp man whose shirt sleeves were always doubled neatly back from his wrists and whose eyes twinkled with an awry chipper little smile that glinted with two gold teeth under a tidy patch of a mustache. Abdullah was himself a Palestinian whose family had owned farm lands and orchards around Jerusalem before 1967: "We had then food to eat from our fields," he had reminisced one afternoon, driving back to the hotel. "We grew ourselves the vegetables and the fruit, but here now I have nothing—no land, no house that is mine, no cash in the bank, my wife is sue-ing all the clo-thes. I am sick, I work anyway. Yes, is true. Cash for everything here, yes"— he briefly scrubbed his fingertips together—"even for the mints in the tea." But although two of his six sons were members of the Lion Cubs, Abdullah himself maintained a cheerful careful neutrality among the array of Palestinian commando groups in Amman. "I find out about them all first, listen to what each one have to say, so then I am able to decide in my mind which one the best, yes?" His research, so far, had been under way for over three years, while he had attended to a steady succession of journalists, from Bonn to Los Angeles, whose cards he always carried in his wallet like a plump hip-pocket album of citations and pleasant memories. But now, on the way to the fedayeen office in Amman where they would get clearance to go on to Irbid, he mentioned hurriedly, tonelessly, almost in a vague embarrassment, with his askew little smile, "Is better you not cross with them, yes. From the bank, you see everything—true, yes, no need to cross." And the American wondered, *What has he sniffed*, his uneasiness only gathering dimension when, in the office of the group's command right before they set out, small hot glasses of sweet tea were distributed around and then raised and sipped with what seemed a grave formality, as if he were partaking of some secret ceremony.

Then they were climbing the steep slopes north out of Amman—an abrupt breathtaking disclosure, like a map rapidly unfolded before them, of high ridges, vast windy spaces—while the car radio played Palestinian propaganda hymns angelically sung by a children's chorus. At midmorning, they stopped for lemonade at Jarash, sitting on the open porch of a café that overlooked a weedy field of Roman ruins, a monumental rubble of bleak stones in broom sage and muffling heat: everywhere in the Middle East, it seemed, was this litter of prodigious past presences, and each time it was astonishing that there was once such rapt enterprise and ambition in such heat. Then, they reached a sweeping plateau of tawny blond fields under an immense sky clouded a molten grayish blue—an overwhelming coolly blowing emptiness with only a flimsy line of telephone poles, an occasional tattering Bedouin tent, and once a clanking herd of goats shuffling across the highway's meaningless intrusion of pavement—and finally he saw in the distance the faint thin clutter of a town: Irbid.

Reaching the outskirts, they turned off the road and pulled up at a meager concrete house plopped down isolate and shadeless in the center of a treeless yard of oil-stained dirt scattered with rusting motor parts, axles and mufflers, with several jeeps and small trucks parked about at peculiar tilts and slumps. Suddenly a fedayee stepped around a corner from the rear of the house, his submachine gun leveled at them—*Here? So quickly, trivially?*—and Abdullah with a casual discreet alacrity opened the door and got out while simultaneously engaging the fedayee in a barking exchange. The fedayee finally nodded and slightly lowered his submachine gun, and took them then around the back to a small cement room, furnished with the inevitable haphazard chairs and battered desks, where more of them were gathered, slouched low in their chairs, regarding the entry of Abdullah and the American with only incidental glances. An older man sitting behind one of the desks was describing with a grinning leer an encounter with Jordanian troops the night before, talking to a woman among them whom the American had seen once before in the organization's office in Amman. She had announced to him then that she was a Belgian journalist, a Trotskyite, whose husband was a government minister back in Brussels; a towering and gangling figure with a long drooping mulish face and large square teeth, she was pale and sallow of make-up, her lank hair whacked off like a shingle at the back of her neck, her round bulbed eyes giving her a look of lugubrious alertness. Outfitted now in guerrilla duds with a canteen belt and heavy new yellow boots, she listened, leaning slightly forward, as the fedayee told her, "They said to us we could not cross because there was shelling. This captain, he said, 'I do not care who you are, we are letting no one through!' In a very sharp voice, you know—very much authority. I said to him, 'Be more polite—we will take your weapons as we did before. Be more polite. . . .'" With this, the woman whooped—drew her knees together with a peculiarly awkward feminine delicacy and slapped them with her large flat hands: "Oh, but they are so *timid!* I cannot believe it. What can you do with such an army? They will not *engage.* They are absolutely useless. Absolutely *useless. . . .*"

Abdullah had found himself a chair in a far corner where he was leisurely chatting now with the fedayeen around him; the American was beginning to feel he had simply been noticed and then forgotten, until Abdullah abruptly turned to him with the faces of the others in the room unanimously turning with his, regarding the American with bemused gazes while Abdullah told him, "They say Israeli planes bombing all this morning, so we wait a little while, is too dangerous now." With that, the woman peered at him; "Oh, you didn't bring any equipment? You must at least take a gun, you know. I never go on these operations unarmed." For some reason, he sensed she was assuming a custodial air toward him. "No," he said, "I'm just a journalist, I don't—" and she said with a sniff, "Well, they always take very good care of you, anyway. But I assure you, you would be better off with at least a side arm. I take always a Kalashnikov myself, and I have had to use it a number of times, believe me."

Another fedayee entered the room with a shallow white box under his arm—a squat swarthy youth with a whorled ducktail and sideburns in the original vintage hillbilly honky-tonk style. He quickly crossed the room, with a kind of lunging swagger, to a chair onto which he precipitously dropped himself, leaning forward awkwardly from the edge with humped shoulders and hung head, which, after a deep breath, swung about to the others with a shy smile, the box still clamped under his arm. "Ah, this one, now," the woman muttered to the American, "this one is the sniper—their sharpshooter. He's only just gotten out of the hospital, he was wounded in the stomach. . . ." The youth, suddenly realizing she was talking about him, looked at her sweetly and witlessly as she murmured on to the American, "He has an almost seraphic face, don't you think?" She suddenly got up and moved across the room to stand over him; he gazed up at her innocently and happily as she gave his cheek a brief soft pinch and said, "Your wound, let us see—your *wound*, your—" and she manfully slapped her own flat brass-buckled stomach until he finally understood her and, glancing around at his comrades with a furtive grin, pulled up his shirt to reveal a stale sour bandage wrapped around his belly. "My

God," the woman trilled, "but why don't you *clean* it? You can't just go on leaving it like that, don't you realize?" He merely swiped his knuckles under his nose, across his grin, blinking up at her and nodding vaguely. "All of them," she boomed to the American, "they're just like children; they have no idea how to take proper care of themselves," and there was a general exchange of grins in the room as she went over to her knapsack, pulled out a comb, returned to the youth, and began fiercely combing his hair back from his forehead, one large hand fluttering after each vicious pull, while he simply looked around at his comrades in helpless delight. "Look at this, just coated with dust," she burbled. "Doesn't he ever wash it? Like the coat of a mongrel, I tell you. Oh—" and gave it up, tapping his neck with the comb: "Impossible!" She plopped back down in her chair, blowing a limp thread of hair from her cheek, and then, her voice tripping again down to low confidential register, informed the American, "I think fourteen, fifteen he has gotten. Incredible marksman. But of course, they never talk about that business; it's not a matter of heroics or anything for them. It is just what they have to do, like a job. They are marvelously natural about it all. . . ."

A moment later, the youth left with the white box under his arm, and after a few minutes returned, attired now in an iridescent blue shirt, patterned in diamonds, with white buttons sewn to the fold of the short sleeves, to the flaps of the pockets, and to the flaring collar tips. He was instanly greeted with yowls, yodels, hoots, whistles. He plunged sidewise down into the nearest chair, his grin paling a little bit, becoming a half-hearted semblance of the delight of a moment before, and finally vanished altogether; even after the bedlam had subsided, he continued to sit in a faint bewildered sulk, his eyes dulled. "Poor thing," the woman whispered to the American. "But it is a rather gorgeous shirt for a sniper, isn't it? Of course, he has a job in the daytime where he has to work very close to the river and the Israelis, so he has to have something to wear other than his commando uniform. If they had any idea of who he was and how many of them he has killed—perhaps fourteen of them. But wait, would you like to know exactly the number? Let me ask—" The youth merely looked at her vacantly after her question, and then turned to a fedayee beside him for a translation. Then, after the translation, he shrugged, delivered a long rapid answer, and then turned and gazed out of a window while his answer was translated: "He says he does not know, he cannot remember all of the times—maybe two, three, four, he is not sure, but no more than that. Anyway, he says, he is only like all of us, only fighting to liberate Palestine and to make for a just society in Palestine. It is not that he is wanting to kill persons; it is not important how many there may have been, for no one hates the Jews; it is a war against Zionist imperialism. . . ." But even when the translator was finished, the youth continued gazing out of the window, leaning forward with one hand propped on his knee, his face absolutely empty. "You see how modest they all are about it?" the woman murmured to the American. "He has gotten at least fifteen, I know that, but you ask him and he tells you only two or three." There was a long silence in the room. Finally someone spoke, and there was a shifting in the chairs, a slight laughter, and the youth turned at last from the window. But still did not look at anyone, hunched forward on the edge of his chair and gazing at the floor, as if abruptly detached, sunk in some profound remoteness from which he only glimpsed up now and then as someone laughed. And eventually, without a word, he got up and left the room.

Here, then, the American waited, hearing now and then the distant crowing of a rooster, as the morning mellowed into noon. Once there was a shout from outside, and everyone instantly scrambled up and scattered out into the yard where, separate and motionless, they stood looking up at the sky while two fedayeen in a nearby foxhole furiously cranked and wheeled an anti-aircraft gun's muzzle upward. But all he could detect was a faint keening in the sky, perhaps three small light distant thumps: nothing more—a remote murmur that shortly vanished again into the morning's stillness. Then, from a nearby rusted oil drum of smoldering ashes into which someone had tossed a handful of small-caliber shells, there came a muffled popping, at which he flinched, and he thought, *Could it be I have come six thousand miles to be assassinated by a trash can? . . .*

They lingered for a while in the yard, and one of the guerrillas presently threw his arm around a friend and told him something as he nodded toward the woman who was standing with them, and then watched her, a grin cocked on his face, his feet impatiently shuffling, as his friend translated: "He says he wants to know if you have a girl friend you could maybe fix him up for a date maybe—" and the woman placed her hands on her hips, put one foot forward, and glanced away from them, the corners of her mouth pulled down in genuine aggrievement: "Well, now, that is very nice. How wonderful—" She continued wagging her head up and down. "What am I supposed to be, a dating bureau for everybody here?" At that there was an exchange of elbowed nudges, good-natured disclaiming guffaws, which did not seem to reassure her noticeably, and she merely kept staring off at nothing in particular, standing in that slouch with her hands on her hips.

Back inside the room, the hours passed in a sporadic locker-room play and banter. One tall and drowsy-eyed youth came and was immediately goosed by a comrade sitting by the door; he wheeled with a quick hopping jig and simply slapped the wall as someone else leaned forward and jabbed, and he wheeled again with that frenzied shuffle, slapping a table: this ritual continued—jab, hop-slam!—to inexhaustible brays of laughter on into the afternoon. The American noticed one pudgy boy, not more than thirteen, lounging morosely in a far corner with a Kalashnikov slung over his shoulder, smoking a cigarette: "Yes, him, he was with another organization," he was told, "but someone there spoke harshly to him once, treated him roughly, so he came to us and asked if he could join our people. That was about six months ago, and he has been with us ever since." Then, for a while, they idly pitched pistols back and forth for inspection, flipping out the chambers, then opening desk drawers and scrabbling out fistfuls of bullets, which they carefully snicked, their mouths briefly pursing, into each socket. Pulling out one drawer, someone came across a framed picture which was passed to the American—a smoggy photograph of a rumpled youth leaning with a squinting smile against a tree in some bleak illumination (something, indeed, oddly familiar and evocative about that blank white glare) ; not quite two hours after this photographed instant of his obliging grin in the sun-shine, he was dead, a land mine having blown off both his feet. His picture, encased now in a white plastic dime-store frame, was reverently passed on around the room, each of them holding it for a long solemn gaze, and then was returned to the desk drawer.

They brought the American something to eat, setting it on the edge of a desk beside him; large flat flaps of bread and a tin bowl in which there was heaped a kind of chicken hash cooked in water, the bristly neck and beaked head of a rooster lying on top of it. As soon as Abdullah noticed it, he stood up and turned to the fedayee in charge of the office, a thin and scruffy youth named Nadia, and began talking to him in a low mutter, with that sober glaze on his face again of negotiating uneasy balances, and finally turned to the American: "I tell him this not be good for your stomach, you have been having trouble with your stomach, so I take you into town, find something for you there. He says is all right, he understand." The youth, Nadia, then stood and, placing his hand lightly on the American's shoulder, caught his eyes in a peculiar tender gaze, with a broad smile showing a stumpy row of yellow tarred teeth: "Don worry. Don worry. Is O.K. . . ." And suddenly the American sensed some gentle and almost sweet solicitude around him, some elaborate studied deference that had been proceeding, actually, all through the morning—a puzzling, vaguely uncomfortable officiousness. None of them, it seemed, would look him for very long in the eye, and those times he had returned from a stroll outside, he would walk into a sudden hush in the room; they would all look away when he glanced at them. Even Abdullah seemed to conspire in this careful politeness now, seemed to be regarding him from some deliberate and strangely formal distance. At the restaurant in town, Abdullah immediately arranged for a bottle of arak to be brought to him in a brown paper bag for that dull inward pinch in his stomach which had become now a small abiding fact of his condition through each day, and when the meal was finally set before them, Abdullah inquired softly, "Is maybe the fan blowing too strong?"

"No, it's all right. It feels fine."

"But maybe you don't like so strong a breezes while you eat.

I will turn it just some little bit, you tell me if that is better. . . ."

But when they returned to the fedayeen office and Abdullah, after a short conversation with Nadia, turned to tell him the planes were still bombing the road to the river, "Is too danger-ous to go yet, we wait here yet for a time and then see," the American heard himself suddenly blurting, "But, look, it doesn't matter to me. I'm not worried if they're not. They can't spare me risks they take themselves. I didn't come here for that. Why don't we go on now?" And Nadia, with a slightly harried smile, said, "No, no. Is not safe now, we wait. You must be easy. . . ." After a moment, one of the fedayeen began talking to the woman. She nodded, and then looked at the American: "He was asking me if you have any political opinions, if you are one of them?"

Both the fedayee and the woman were watching him now with an almost ravenous expectancy, their eyes level. "You told them I was a journalist?" he said at last. "Yes, of course. He knows that. But he asked if you had any political opinions, if you are also Marxist-Leninist, and I told him I didn't know, that I would ask you. . . ." He felt a vague dizziness; had again that uneasy sensation of something reaching for his hand. "Tell him—tell him I am not necessarily Marxist-Leninist—I mean that no dogma—I don't necessarily belong to any orthodoxy, but —tell him I understand that his people suffer, I understand their anger, I am—I am sympathetic, tell him that. But I am a writer, and I believe that life is larger than any particular political system, so my opinions are not of any particular doc-trine. . . ." He dangled a moment longer, then simply leaned back. The woman translated, and the fedayee listened; he paused a moment and then said something else to her. She turned to the American: "But he wants to know if you are with them." *Hellfire*, he thought, *what is going on here?* He said, "It's not—I am not here like that. I am certainly not here against the Palestinians, you can tell him that. But I am here as a writer," and he waited as she translated this, swiping at a buzz of flies in front of his face. This time the fedayee did not look at him. When she had finished, he merely slapped his hand on the table like a dismissal, and began talking to the others in the room, his voice suddenly loud and jovial.

An hour later, someone came in and announced the driver had arrived to take them to the river. As he got up to leave, gathering in a deep breath, he looked back at Abdullah, who was sitting quietly in a chair against a far wall, turned sidewise with his legs crossed and his arm slung over the back. "Look, Abdullah, why don't you come on with us?" he said, and Abdullah seemed to flush slightly. "No, no," he answered hurriedly, grinning and tapping two fingers against his temple as he cast amiable glances around at the others in the room. "I be afraid, I stay here. I wait for you at hotel in town. You get back tonight, I drive you on to Amman, yes, or you wait until the morning, whichever you want. I stay here, be ready to take you back, yes. Is best."

As they set out now in the dusk, he felt a sensation of release. The woman—her head wrapped in a kerchief and her voice a little brittle and tinkling—was sitting in the back seat of the Land Rover between him and the lank fedayee who had earlier performed the solemn jigs at his comrades' pokings, with Nadia up front beside the driver. They battered on through Irbid, passing evening sidewalks filled with people, Nadia and the fellow in the back seat holding their Kalashnikovs as they wheeled urgently around the square before the stares of the townfolk under the soft white sky of dusk, *Ah, so they will know we are going to the river,* Nadia flinging salutes to girls at corners, friends who grinned and shouted to them from cafés and chairs in front of the open doors of garages, *Well, it really isn't a bad life; what else have they ever had to replace moments like this?* and finally on out into the open darkening fields of the evening with solitary glimmers of light under a huge lonesome sky. They stopped briefly at a small crossroads store, and the long loping sleepy-eyed fellow in the back got out and then quickly returned with a paper bag, clambering back in the Land Rover with a jubilant hoot, "We get beer now. O.K.?" and placing the bag on the floorboard between his feet as the Land Rover churned back into the road. Passing now through wind flushes of warmth and chill, the American realized there was in his throat a dumb involuntary exultation. The fedayee in the back seat began withdrawing from the bag large green quart bottles of Petra beer, offering one to the woman; she received it a bit gingerly, foam spilling down her hand as her other hand clutched the bar across the front seat, a certain quietness having settled over her now, only chirping thinly as they spanked over a dip in the road, "Oh . . . my . . ." After the beer, the fedayee produced oranges, distributing them around as the car began ·plunging down looping curves, through successive wellings of warmth, with the night's inhaled scents now subtly nipped with that brief dry ammoniac muskiness of deserts at night, that tang of dust touched by dew. Nadia suddenly withdrew his pistol at one curve with a cry, "Look! That bridge!" aiming it hastily at a viaduct on a moonlit slope beside them: the crack! crack! was instantly sucked away without echo by the wind, a short fleeting blotted sound repeated twice. "When I get out of that office," Nadia shouted into the back seat, "I am always glad. . . ." The American turned and, above the uptilting bottle of the fedayee discovered the sudden solitary appearance of the moon hovering in the limpid violet sky. Turning in the front seat, Nadia looked up: "Ah, good moon. Good moon." He took a gleeful bite out of his orange, and grinned. "I finish eating, then I hunt." A moment later, he pointed over the windshield of the Land Rover to the dark shape of a mountain ahead— "Star of the Wind, that mountain"—and suddenly, beyond the mountain, the American saw, in the far distance, scattered drifts of lights like an indistinct glimmering pollen. "And there, the kibbutzim!" Nadia announced, but with an impersonal enthusiasm, like a tourist guide pointing out some feature of novel interest.

Reaching the floor of the valley, only some fifty yards now from the Jordan River, their voices sank to whispers as the Land Rover eased with its lights out along a dirt road between willow plumes and canebrakes through a violent oppressive heat. Then, rounding a curve, the American saw on a slight slope ahead of them a Moslem village, huddled soundless and lightless under the moon, and as they slowly pulled into one of its streets, he discovered it was absolutely empty of inhabitants, a ghost village filled with rubble under a quick noise-less swooping and flutter of bats. The Land Rover stopped, and Nadia left with his Kalashnikov to look around. "Do you suppose there are any of them here?" the woman suddenly muttered, sitting motionless now in the back seat with her two hands clutching the bar in front of her. "We were supposed to have gotten here this morning, you know. I think we should decide something. Why has he left us just stranded in this jeep in full—" But then Nadia was standing above them in the dirt street, waving them after him. They walked for several minutes through the town, past windows through which the American saw moonlight spilling over fallen ceilings, and then along a narrow passage between two toppled walls—and he sensed first, before he actually discerned, a soft scamper of figures around them. They stopped finally in a small courtyard between four houses, and now the figures began emerging from the dark doorways around them, submachine guns slung over their shoulders, gathering around the American and the woman as Nadia quietly talked to one of them, and bringing with them a different whiff in the night, close and metallic and rank, like sweat on rusting iron. One of them, standing directly in front of the American, struck a match in his cupped hands to light a cigarette, and as he did he fixed the American in a sudden imperious stare, savage and glaring and spectral—like some furious wordless beckon, invitation, of rage—and then he realized Nadia was talking to him, ". . . Not going across tonight. . . ," watching the face now dimming out before him as the match flame diminished, sighed back into itself, the face dully receding again into the dark. Nadia continued, ". . . So no operation. Same with everybody. Not tonight."

So they drove instead down the road along the river, and now the American took a bottle of beer and lifted it in long deep tepid gulps, the glass rapping his teeth, his hands finally wet and dripping, as they passed a succession of forsaken blind-windowed Moslem villages, the Land Rover's headlights still extinguished and the woman only trilling once, "Now, what? You mean we're just going to drive along like this for the rest of the night?" and then subsiding into a rigid silence. "We must be careful," Nadia said from the front seat. "We might have accidents with Jordanian army. They had very serious accident just here last night—" and the woman confided with a low hiss, "Accident, yes. That's their euphemism for a confrontation, you know. Accidents like dashing down a road at night with no lights on in full view of the enemy just across the river; accidents like that they don't count. Incredible."

They were stopped only once at a Jordanian checkpoint; the soldier peered for a moment at the American in the back seat and then said something, and the American answered with a curious jubilant elation, "I'll tell you, I don't speak a word of Arabic. I don't know one bloody syllable of it. . . ." On down the road, Nadia turned and told him, "They always want to know do we have mortars. That was what he ask you, if you have mortar." They passed occasional dark and anonymous figures on the side of the road, and finally were waved over by three guerrillas in berets who, after a short conversation with Nadia, jumped in the rear of the Land Rover: "Al Saqai," explained Nadia, "from Syria. They have someones on the other side now, need to find their driver again—" and shortly they came to an ambulance that was parked on a narrow trail leading off down toward the river, with a man standing beside it in a white smock, smoking a cigarette. The Land Rover heaved to a stop, and the three Saqai commandos leaped out, Nadia joining them as they talked to the man, who kept taking ragged puffs from his cigarette as he gestured fitfully toward the river. Nadia then returned to the Land Rover, and as it lurched on down the road he said, "He is a doctor, he says two commandos still across the river for several hours now; he is very worried, you could see. . . ."

The sleepy-eyed youth on the other side of the woman now began pressing her to take a swig from his bottle. At last she accepted, one fastidious sip, and promptly returned it to him, resuming her rigid, erect pose, her back not quite touching the seat behind her, staring silently straight ahead with her kerchief still tied futilely over her hopelessly blown hair, both hands grimly grasping the bar before her. Presently they came to a collision that had apparently happened only moments before—two upended and crumpled trucks lying some ten yards apart on the same side of the road—and the Land Rover slowed to a stop, Nadia and his two comrades quickly scrambling out. "What is this, now?" the woman chirped. "What are they doing?" From a ditch by one of the trucks, she and the American could hear subdued shouting. "Well, so here we sit," the woman muttered, "right in the middle of the road, absolutely motionless and exposed. Oh, wonderful. See how rational they are? Absolutely fantastic. Can you believe they are trying to make a revolution? Incredible. Absolutely no discipline—an accident, everybody gets out—no planning; they don't know what they're doing from one minute to the next. Impossible, I tell you. . . ." Finally two Jordanian soldiers each brought to the Land Rover a large plastic bag containing something heavy and shapeless, unrecognizable, hefting the bags up into the rear and then climbing in to sit beside them. With a single glance back over her shoulder, the woman muttered, "Oh, my God. Those are the bodies, I suppose," and then merely fixed her stare straight ahead again, only tilted further forward now. As the Land Rover set off down the road, the American found his own nostrils involuntarily dreading but seeking an alien whiff from behind him, but in the hot night air there were only dusty hints of sagebrush. The soldiers, with their loads, were deposited at a crossroads, and the woman asked in a somewhat faltering voice, "Nadia, I suppose those were the bodies, weren't they?" and Nadia turned with a grin. "No, no, just weapons. Weapons from the crash . . ." But the American found himself not altogether certain.

Then, as they were making their way back down the road, the

Land Rover suddenly careened, and the American saw another jeep looming in front of them, an instant now of slow terrific motion, the other jeep seeming to drift for a moment inches off their fender, and he heard the woman beside him emitting a sound like a dull lowing as the Land Rover continued to swerve with a kind of sluggish deliberation, laboring, and they missed —skidding wildly to a stop some fifteen yards apart. Immediately, Nadia grabbed his Kalashnikov and leaped into the middle of the road, his feet spraddled and one arm gesturing in the moonlight as he howled at the jeep; the American called to him, "Now, wait a minute, Nadia. Come on, you don't want to be starting something here twenty yards from the river, and with your own fellows. . . ."

With a last flourish of his arm, Nadia returned to the Land Rover, and after a few moments, as they were proceeding on down the road, the woman merely murmured, "They are unbelievable. Unbelievable." Then the Land Rover began to sputter, faltered, and at last expired, and the sleepy-eyed youth alighted, threw up the hood, and performed some unseen ministrations until the motor clattered back to at least a semblance of its former energy. But after another half-mile, it again gagged, both the youth and the driver now gathering under its raised hood for a muffled consultation. From that point on, it proceeded uncertainly, like a wound toy, from one mechanical administration to the next—in head-snapping yanks, its backfiring rather hair-raising claps of noise in the stillness— and the woman pronounced with a small light laugh, her head tossing with each halting hiccup of the engine, "There you— God!—are. Even their machines—God!—are irrational. . . ."

All the while, across the river, confronting this blunderous hectic pratfalling slapstick plunging back and forth on the

Jordanian bank, there continued the innocent twinkling of the kibbutzim lights: as remote and alien, it seemed now, as if they were another century, another continent. From this side, they seemed strangely intimidating and serene. And the American remembered the expression on the Jordanian soldier's face that morning at the bridge, only a few days ago, when he had seen the man, the last prisoner released by the Israelis; it was before he appeared, while the other prisoners were still coming across—a Jordanian guard standing off to himself along the bridge's railing, watching the Israeli officers pacing jauntily back and forth with that buoyant bounce from their toes, his face lost in a long glower of sullen impotent rage, finally taking his cigarette from his mouth and flinging it, with a savage lash of his hand, into the river.

He had finished another beer now, but still a dreariness hung over his spirit. The dull pinch in his innards that had accompanied him ever since Egypt had now become a vivid burning, and gradually he began to imagine it as the pangs of some inner mayhem, some interior violence worked by the psychic violation of having come too close, out of a whimsical and superficial lust of curiosity, to partaking deeply of a violence, an experience to which he didn't belong—trying to negotiate such a feat of ultimate detachment. He began to suspect this as the secret dread in his hotel room through that long night before: indeed, as the cold premonitory nausea at each small tug and invocation of that romance of death ever since he had been in Jordan—from the professor towering over him against the stars his first night in the city, then his hand suddenly snatched on the stage of the amphitheatre, the wink of the attendant in the hotel corridor when he had left that morning, the ritualistic glasses of tea, Nadia's solicitous smile and lingering hand on his shoulder, that sudden cordial but vaguely proprietary curiosity in the fedayeen office at the end of the afternoon, "You are with us?" all the way up to that moment in the village along the river, the final instant of that carnivorous gaze in the match glow. . . .

At last, they were passing back through Irbid, its streets shuttered now in the dim milky wash of the streetlights, finally reaching the concrete house on the outskirts, the only room lit in the early morning the office where he had passed the day waiting. He stayed outside in the yard, in the dark, as Nadia went in to inquire about Abdullah. Presently Nadia returned to report, "He went somewhere to hotel in town, but nobody knows which one. We call hotels now, you come in and wait." Following Nadia on inside to the office, the American discovered, standing in the exact center of the room under its unshaded light bulb, a hulking and shabby vagabond, bald save for a soft tuft of pale hair on the top of his head, and eyebrowless, with pale vague lashes over small pale eyes: a massive materialization out of the plains of this night, sandaled, with heavy arms like those of a Suma wrestler, monumentally impassive, inscrutable, but yet with some peculiar air of absolute authority about him. While the few fedayeen who were still in the office watched him with a deferential attentiveness, he slowly unscrewed the cap to his canteen—and then spoke, in his voice some unknown accent, Viennese or Slavic or possibly Finnish: "On the bottom is Damascus water. Above that is Beirut water. Above that Baghdad water. And on the top is —let's see—" He turned up the canteen and took a long deliberate swallow: "Ah—Amman water." *He must be some wandering Marxist commissar,* the American thought, *some itinerant adventurer without nationality, without even origin,* and then the fantasy stole over him out of the deep pit of the night, *Ah. So here he is. This is him. The son of a bitch himself—Death, disguised as a knapsacked vagabond revolutionary.* . . . (And three months later, back in America, he instantly remembered this figure standing under that unshaded light bulb at two in the morning, in the fedayeen office in Irbid, as from the den of his home in an Atlanta suburb he watched newsreels of the killings, dimensionless and miniaturized on the screen of the television set, that ensued in that land not long after he left it.)

"We have to drive to look for your driver," Nadia told him. "We try the hotels, nobody answer. You want maybe, you can sleep with us here tonight, then find him in the morning. Or maybe there be operation tomorrow, and you come—" But the American was already on his feet; his compulsion now was to withdraw as quickly as possible—bodily, emotionally, totally—from all of it. To leave. Then, as Nadia started the Land Rover and turned it toward the highway, he heard behind them a loud whoop, and looked back to see the woman standing alone in the middle of the dark yard, calling after them, "Hal-lee, Nadia. Oh, Nadia—" her voice gallantly robust again with only the slightest crack of uncertainty in its brave honking hail: "Hal-lee, Nadia. Where are you going? What is supposed to happen to me now? . . ."

They finally found Abdullah's car parked on a side street. Mounting a skinny flight of stairs, he and Nadia roused the night-desk man, who stood swaying just a little with his nightshirt stuffed into beltless trousers while Nadia asked him to awaken Abdullah. Then Nadia turned to the American and extended his hand to say farewell, and, with a diminishing clatter of footsteps down the stairs, was gone. The American sat now on a bench against the wall, the long wainscoted room like the lobby of some old frontier boarding house, and hung now in a silence, the emptiness and stillness of those hours of night from the other side of the moon. After a while, there was a mumbling from somewhere. The night clerk reappeared and told him, his voice echoing up and down the length of the room, "You driver come now. Say wait just one minute." Behind his desk again, he watched the American for several minutes, and observed with a smile, "Back to Amman, eh?" The American merely nodded at him. And presently Abdullah appeared, fully dressed with his shirt sleeves doubled neatly back from his wrists, but still somewhat stumbly with sleep, blinking gamely against his bleariness, struggling to muster some measure of briskness again. "O.K., ready, no, fine, all right—I get two, three hours sleep, I'm fine now. You not go across, much more wise, yes. So we go back to Amman. . . ."

And as they descended now softly down through the vast mountains of the night, the American stretched out on the back seat, his arm over his eyes. In a few hours it would be day again, that simple peaceful certainty delivered out of darkness and chaos, and he would be leaving, flying to that other side, that other world that he had seen across the river. The pain in his midsection now was only a little duller, but at last he slept.

III

The Other Side of the River

And the Lord spake unto Moses, saying, send thou
men, that may search the land of Canaan, which I give
unto the children of Israel. . . . And they returned
from searching of the land after forty days. . . . And
they spake unto all the company of the children of
Israel, saying, The land, which we passed through to
search it, is an exceeding good land. If the Lord
delight in us, then he will bring us into this land, and
give it us; a land which floweth with milk and honey.

HIS FIRST ACTUAL GLIMPSE of them had been while he
was still on the Arab side—that morning at the bridge when he
had seen the man, the last one of the prisoners whose release
by the Israelis he and other journalists had been brought there
by the Jordanian press ministry to witness.

Only some fifteen yards away—across the makeshift span of
rough wooden planks and rusted girders which had replaced
the original Allenby Bridge—he watched, as he waited for the
trucks with the prisoners to arrive, three Israeli soldiers standing
in the shade of eucalyptus trees in front of their guard post,
striking a pose of almost calculated magnificent languorousness,
hips casually slanted, arms crossed with their UZI submachine
guns slung over their shoulders, now and then raising one hand
to chew briefly on a thumbnail and then spit tightly, precisely

to one side. Behind them, from a high rocky butte in the distance, a somewhat oversized Israeli flag—that simple star insignia of deep blue on white that suggests a medical banner, clean and chaste and almost clinical—flowed spectacularly like an abiding assertion against a pure blue desert sky over territory they had taken in 1967. Before he had left the United States, a friend of his, an army colonel, had said, "You know, all these things we've heard over here about the Israelis, what they did in 1967—it's just hard to believe they're all that good. You'd think they were supermen," and he thought now, *So that's them, at last. The other side: to the Arabs, alien invading marauders versed in the magic of the new technological century, unvanquishable, abruptly arrived out of the West to colonize them from the Nile to the Euphrates; but back home—after all those Sunday School mornings in brick Baptist churches in small Southern cities, and, too, the wan ashen newsreels of Dachau and Buchenwald—the legendary heirs of Joshua and Gideon who have accomplished after four thousand years the second Exodus. So that's what they look like. . . .* Their sleeves rolled above their elbows, they would occassionally amble a few steps and then pause, cuffing the dust with their boots, tamping and tidying it with their toes, like football players on the sidelines before a game, as they peered for a moment with a kind of vague bemusement at the turmoil of soldiers and journalists and photographers on the other side of the bridge.

At last, the trucks with the prisoners arrived, accompanied by several jeeps bearing Israeli officers. With that, a Jordanian brigadier general walked out to the middle of the bridge—a long gaunt greyhound of a figure, with a hatchet-hacked face, who had been maintaining a resolutely cheerful and benign manner as he waited, chatty and even whimsical, with the parents of his English wife on hand to witness the occasion. After a moment, an Israeli officer, short and chunky and wearing a beret, came briskly striding out to meet him with a jaunty taut bounce from his toes, hailing him with a shout, *"Good morning, sir! How are you?* Good to see you again—" They shook hands, exchanging a few fleeting pleasantries with one or two short laughs, never quite looking at each other. The Jordanian general then proposed a few details for the transaction, standing at a slight droop as he amiably motioned with the papers in his hand, and the Israeli officer—a Major Horowitz— listened with quick pistonlike pumps and wags of his head, his hands clamped his sides in a stance of briefly arrested haste and urgency, merely chewing his lower lip now and then, giving quick sidewise flips of one hand as he snapped, "As you wish. . . . As you wish. . . . No problem, Brigadier. . . . O.K., fine with us. . . ." The other officers who had come with him, booted like paratroopers with their sleeves also rolled above their elbows, stood off to one side along the railing of the bridge in a graceful languid almost feline slouch, hips canted and hands propped on their low-slung canteen belts, their caps tipped forward over their eyes, and the American, watching them, thought, *My God, they manage to swagger just standing still. . . .*

By now, the congregation of journalists and soldiers on the Jordanian side had also spilled onto the bridge, surrounding Horowitz and the general, and finally, after an exasperated perusal of this untidiness, Horowitz went over to his other officers for a whispered consultation, returning to the general and gesturing with an open palm toward the crowd, hunching his shoulders, "Excuse me, Brigadier, sorry, but we've kept our people back off the bridge. I really must ask—" With the papers in his hand, the general made a few affable ineffectual shooing waves at the throng. The officers along the railing now began stalking back and forth fretfully, scuffing the bridge planks with light kicks of their boots, regarding the disorderliness around Horowitz with repeated looks of fine distaste. But Horowitz, for his part—with two Jordanian soldiers now at his side only some inches away from him—occupied himself with idly rubbing his cheek downward while he cast glances at them over his shoulder, swiftly eyed them up and down as if absorbed in some private oblique appraisal, totally measuring and dismissing them in one brief curious summary stare, after which, the American noticed, the soldiers looked away uncomfortably: *What he's doing is casing them. Every one of them. He's looking to see if there's any sign they might have gotten any better since he last saw them. And they know it, they know what he's doing. . . .*

Two of the officers, kneeling now and looking over the side of the bridge, suddenly called to Horowitz, and when he went over to them, they pointed out a loose bolt in the understructure. Horowitz then called over the general—the Jordanian army, it seemed, still had responsibility for the bridge's maintenance—and showed him the loose bolt, announcing, "We thought you might want to look to this, Brigadier." The general stood very still for an instant, peering down at the dangling bolt, his arms hanging limply at his sides with the release papers still in one hand. Then he lifted his head and, gazing off into space, announced rather loudly, "Well, I don't think this is really the moment to be discussing such a matter," turning abruptly and going back to where the prisoners were being processed, a faintly harried expression on his gaunt beaked face. *They win them all,* the American thought. *They're on all the time. They don't let a one go by—but then, maybe they can't afford to. . . .* And he noticed then the Jordanian soldier standing apart from everyone else on the bridge, absolutely motionless, his shirt sleeves, unlike the Israelis', buttoned around his wrists in the heat, which gave him somehow that peculiar appearance of sulky dowdiness that the American remembered in those children long ago in school who came from the shacky neighborhoods of town; a solitary brooding figure absorbed in watching the chipper bouncing saunter and prowl of the Israelis before him with a glare of mute helpless outrage, finally taking the cigarette he was smoking and, with a whip of his hand, flinging it into the river.

Pilgrims

DURING THOSE WEEKS among the Arabs, that had been his only glimpse of them. But when at last he left Amman, beginning the flight to Athens from where he would fly on into Tel Aviv, he felt he would somehow be returning in Israel to familiar inflections and perspectives: it would be like stepping back through a looking glass, out of a left-handed world into a right-handed one again. In a sense, it seemed to him, Israel had always been an American experience. When his plane lifted from the Athens airport, he found the cabin now filled almost exclusively with middle-aged checker-coated Jewish dentists and clothing merchants and professors from Cincinnati and Houston and Seattle, with their dumpling-like wives in frosted bouffants and beaded glass chains, along with a large gusty troupe of Protestant preachers crowing happily and continuously to each other high now over the Aegean isles, loudly celebrating all novelties around them and outside the windows in the plain dauntless good corncob accents of Arkansas and Indiana and Oklahoma, one among them regularly indulging himself, at every pass of the stewardess, in a modest "Yippee-yi-ohhhh-kiyea!" Though he was still weeks away from the States, in this hermetic jet cabin the American had a sudden sensation, like a false dawn, of being home. At the least, it was a convocation, a collective pilgrimage which in itself comprehended the peculiar folk communion, beyond official government policies, which the United States has with Israel—a special relationship, it seems, America has with no other country save probably England.

Because how else to account, he pondered now as the plane passed over the Mediterranean, for a sixteen-year-old goyische cracker son of a Baptist minister in a musty little outback South Carolina mill town sitting down in his room one mellow autumn night in 1956 and writing a letter to David Ben-Gurion, volunteering his services in the Sinai campaign? All he asked was passage fare and a place afterward in a kibbutz. The fact is, along with innumerable other Americans over the wide fields of his land, the land of Canaan had been the second invisible country of his childhood: he had grown up not only in a small Georgia city along the Savannah River, but in the caves of the prophets along the banks of the Jordan; not only in the vicinity of little piny sawmill communities like Red Hill and Elko, but also in Jericho, Galilee, Mount Carmel, the Sharon Valley. If anything, it was an alter geography which, on Sundays, was more palpable, more *felt,* than the mundane weekday one— abiding changeless and immediate through the years of his father's nomadic pastorates, and therefore in a way the only real one he had ever known. He had recognized some time ago, after passing through renegade seasons of what he fancied to be apostasy and Byronic abandon, that he would always remain secretly and irredeemably a child of the Book. He would always belong to that mythology which had come to him from an old prophet-ridden wasteland of sun and silence (as if God chose

to speak to man only in dust and stillness and impossible heat),
by long-errant improbable translation through the cold moors
and mists of Calvinism, and finally into a violent swampy heat
sensual with honeysuckle halfway around the world, where the
mythology seemed to assume again some aboriginal tragic
authority, really more from the Old Testament than the New.

It was a spiritual hardiness, not alien to grief and doom,
which was, in fact, the common disposition of these ruddy gos-
pel-belt preachers around him now in the plane—they were not
likely to wind up perishing in the Judean desert. Indeed, he was
later to detect a faint ironic bemusement among Israelis with
what had befallen Bishop Pike in his journey there: as if this
uncertain Christian divine, already abstracted through his fastidious equivocations and speculations into a kind of tentative
evanescence, had been simply consumed by the primal glower of
the Judean desert, evaporated with a brief hiss like a singed
spider web. The American himself was to come across similar
souls in the days ahead, pale pilgrims from the far-flung per-
mutations of this region's apocalyptic visions. During a long
drive through Galilee, he and his Israeli guide picked up an
English photographer who had been wandering the country
for weeks assembling a folio of pictures—a long thin willowy
fellow, bulky glasses with lenses like bottle bottoms perched on
a large ponderous nose that drooped over a small wan mouth,
without apparent resources or even change of clothes, but diligently deferential and amiable, with an air of constant muzzy
amazement about him. When they stopped late in the afternoon
at a café in the city of Tiberias, the Englishman, holding his
untasted lemonade while the American and the Israeli driver
tilted their gin-tonics, fell into a brief dispute with the driver
over whether the Sea of Galilee is shaped like a violin or a

harp: the driver began to grow a bit barkish. "Well, I am very sorry, sir, but your information is quite incorrect; it is shaped like a harp," and the Englishman's gentle insistences shortly wisped away altogether in genial and almost contrite accession, "Yes, of course, I'm sure you would know much better than I. Like a harp, is it? I say—" and when a few minutes later he softly ventured, "You know, it surely would be wonderful if perhaps I could accompany you tomorrow when you go up into the Golan Heights," the driver, who by now had reached a peculiar state of passionate complete impatience with the fellow, snapped, "I'm very sorry, but it is impossible. I'm not insured for you. I'm afraid you'll have to find your own way," and the man murmured pleasantly, "Yes, of course, I see. I was only thinking that it would be a wonderful—but certainly, I see." After sundown, they let him out at a dirt road that curved along a slope of the Mount of the Beatitudes to a hostel in the far distance maintained by an Italian religious order; as the car pulled away, the American watched him trudging on down the road, abandoned, a solitary patient diminishing figure in the twilight who suddenly seemed to have a mysterious air about him—a failed cleric, fugitive from some single disastrous moment of weakness, scandal? Fled here in need both of refuge and penance, but nothing actually left for him now but to wander the sites of his lost faith with a camera?

But there still remained everywhere, the American was also to discover, the squat grim edifices left from a quiet time in Christendom, relics of that most formidable pilgrimage of any over the past two thousand years: the Crusaders, blustering profane leek-breathing Frankish knights and Silesian barons who, followed by their drab retinues of monks and priests, undertook to appropriate this alien genesis of their faith with the same brutal simplicity of that faith, like Richard the Lion-Hearted viciously hacking apart the block of stone with his sword. Vanished now, their mad two-hundred-year enterprise—that eccentric improbable adventure—had left behind as their only definitions primitive nameless tombs like Etruscan burial chambers, dim catacombs under Byzantine churches, lit now with a kind of lurid Halloween spookiness, where there still lingers an old rank dampness from their anonymous dreadful endurance and simple bleak savage piety, something infiltrating the nostrils there of dark mortifications and medieval sainthoods, a stale and icy tinge centuries past all warmth and light and life.

All along this American journalist out of the kudzu-hung deeps of the South—whose essential saps had been brewed out of the steams and florid fevers of tent revivals and surging gas-lit hymns—had secretly expected that in reaching Israel he would be negotiating a kind of private exodus of his own, would be returning to the true source of his sensibilities where he would feel he belonged in a way he belonged nowhere else. But on this count, he was to come in the days ahead to a curious distraction. Visiting the presumed progenitive locales of that dramatic ethos in which he had lived for almost twenty years—the birthplace of Jesus, the Garden of Gethsemane—he found them, for the most part, meager token selections of incidental rock enclosed in opulently gilded shrines, cumbersome lavish elaborations of marble columns and scrolled gold-and-jeweled ceilings, sanctuaries muggy with incense and filled with the crinkling voices of tourists in rayon golf shirts and mesh-woven crepe-sole shoes, with a continuous reverent stammering of flash bulbs. "Would you like to pray?" his guide kept whispering in these places, and he kept shaking his head, feeling absolutely nothing, not even curiosity. Another time, pausing at the end of a long ride at a shore-side café under crimson-blooming poinciana trees on the edge of the Sea of Galilee, he sat with his driver under a green-and-orange striped awning slowly sipping a Scotch-and-soda in the quiet blue tints of late afternoon, watching the white-jacketed waiters, at this idle hour with the sun westering low over the dark graphite-blue water around them, fishing with threads and safety pins for Saint Peter's fish while speedboats smacked past pulling skiers, several ancient wooden fishing boats moored nearby with Johnson outboard motors on their sterns nodding dully in the swells. (Later, back in the States, the wife of one Protestant minister widened her eyes when he reported this: "What? On the Sea of Galilee? You mean, water-skiers? . . .")

Jerusalem, however—that old womb of great faiths for half the world, nestled on a height above steep slopes scalloped like oyster shells, a remote cool city of old pale stone and ever-greens that glisten almost black in thin morning mountain sunshine like bright water—still seems to linger in a weather that has a certain religious quality about it, often with a low flanneled autumnal sky above which there lurks smoky glare. The streets themselves are filled with an abstracted diffused translation of that light, in which now there teem all the mingled disciples of those visions annunciated here through the ages: cowled Franciscan friars, bearded Greek Orthodox priests traveling in twos like matched pairs of ravens, Austrian nuns in rimless spectacles floating along in footless white flutterings of cloth, expeditions of flushed women in flowered frocks and paper eyeshades from the Monday-night missionary circles of Methodist churches in Kansas and North Carolina forging resolutely through it all clasping Instamatics and straw handbags, Orthodox Jews with their twined beards and collarless boiled white shirts and black topcoats and wide-brimmed hats evocative somehow of Iowa Amish farmers, with, all the while, the muezzin's languishing imploring howl hovering and fading from nearby towers. But even here, he felt his own religiousness unexpectedly unanswered, dispossessed. One morning he took a cab to that garden where some redoubtable English ecclesiastics, in conjunction with certain of Queen Victoria's Bible-toting generals, concluded that the body of Jesus had been entombed; in what is now a small snug scrupulously tended park of flower beds and meditation benches under cedar trees, a short brisk Scotsman in shirt sleeves was showing around a robed delegation of African matrons, conducting a running commentary with the pleasant glibness of a professional evangelist delivering an informal devotional to the breakfast meeting of a suburban civic club: "But of course, it does not really matter how many other sites there might be where Jesus could have been taken after his crucifixion on Golgatha, because the message of the Scriptures is the same—Jesus Christ *was* crucified on the cross, and on the third day he arose again. We know this absolutely, because if you search the New Testament you will find the unshakable proof of *five hundred* witnesses who saw with their own eyes Christ risen from the dead. . . ." Standing after each announcement at a kind of easy ready attention as his remarks were translated, the guide held his head slightly thrust forward and chin lightly lifted, his short arms straight and rigid at his sides with his curled hands turned palm-backward, a pose of dutiful staunch correctness. But to the journalist, this stubby water-combed cheerful sanitary little Scotsman, along with the raked pathways and tidy flower beds in that fresh Sunday School morning, could not have been more remote from the old original dread and anguish and blood of the event it supposedly enshrined. More obscurely authentic, like a true secret closing of some natural circle, was a simple crude entranceway, discovered along a back lane on the outskirts of Jerusalem one bright windy dusty afternoon; it led down toppling stone steps to a chill dungeonlike grotto lit by a single electric light bulb where, his Arab guide informed him, the mummy-wound corpse of Lazarus had stirred sluggishly back out of death at the rumble of a rolled boulder and sudden shriek of his name above, and where there was now affixed to the damp rock wall a modest wooden plaque like those clumsily lettered signs along Tennessee mountain highways: "PRAISE GOD—JESUS CHRIST Is COMING SOON. ARE YOU READY? IF NOT, ASK HOW TO BE READY—James Andrew, Revival and Healing Center. . . ."

Despite such moments, he found he had arrived with a religious legacy that seemed to have lost its derivations, leaving him with the novel suspended sensation of feeling not only irrelevant but archaic in the Holy Land. But of course, his was a religion, a mythos, which had always been something of an aberration in the primary experience of the region. While in Jerusalem, he took a cab to the Wailing Wall, a titanic loom of blank dull stone tufted at high places with weeds—the only vestige left of that central physicality of the Jewish part: the Temple. Though he arrived there in the empty hours of midafternoon, people were clustered in scatters all along its length—a random assembly of youths in tattered-jean shorts with kerchief headbands and army-surplus knapsacks, other men with ringlets and in calf-length knickers, others in sedate business suits—each one of them, with a strange private oblivious raptness, engaged in a steady urgent dipping and bobbing and shuffling, whispering over small black books, some of them now and then reaching out to touch the wall only a few inches away briefly with their fingertips, as if yet in unbelief and astonishment—an urgent secret palpitation peculiar to come upon out in daylight, in the open. All the while, their moans and supplications and small low cries continued lapping ceaselessly in the quiet afternoon against the immense ancient rock before them, the very subterranean sound of their immeasurable tribulation and endurance echoing now out of all the dark ghettos of their centuries of exile, out of an experience which has been like that of no other people on earth, the phenomenon of their sheer enormous resolution and indestructibility finally inexplicable.

But while they have always seemed a people apart from all others, the Jews—to this particular American at least—had also always seemed most extravagantly characteristic and eloquent of the nature and lot of the whole human species: one degree richer in wit and woe, in civilization and vulgarity, in ethereality and venality, in both gloom and garrulousness. They were an image of the race taken with an extra minute of deep exposure, with a slightly higher resolution, definition, even in their sense of family. (Whenever, as a boy, he had visited the home of a school friend named Hyman Greenfield, he was always conscious in that house of some fuller fragrancy of feeling, some mutual avid awareness among them of each other, at once formal and passionate.) But finally, it had always appeared to him that the Jews, in their two thousand years of exile, had become, more than anything else, eloquent of all mankind's spiritual condition of tentative tenancy and private isolation on this planet; it had come to him before that, in a real sense, all men on this earth are Jews.

It was possible too that what seemed the Jewish identity, the Jewish character, had evolved and embellished itself precisely out of their long sense of universal displacement and homelessness, so that when their homeland was finally regained, it became not so much a normalization as an aberration of their condition. Later, a Jewish teacher was to suggest, "This incredible feat of the Jewish identity surviving two thousand years of exile, it was mainly *because* we had no land—we had to sustain our country among ourselves. But now with Israel, this burden of maintaining a Jewish identity is removed from the Jewish community still abroad, and what that means is that gradually, with those who remain abroad, their Jewishness will dissolve. In effect, we are going to disappear." In some dim way, of course, Portnoy's distress in Israel— "I can't make it in the Promised Land? I can't get it up in the State of Israel?"—may have come from such implications. That spring evening in the West Side apartment before his departure, someone had finally declared, "The truth is Israel is our home, our place—but it seems whenever I go there, I cease to feel Jewish."

And during his first days in Israel, he found he experienced, for similar reasons, the same sensation of dislocation. Not only did he find his own mythology curiously alien in the land of its origin, but also his particular intimate relish for what he had always assumed was the Jewish personality: for one thing, he discovered that, in many of the kibbutzim, there were communal dining halls for all meals, common nurseries where children slept at night away from their parents—all of which seemed to him an uncanny violation of the fierce Jewish sense of family. He mentioned his disconcertion on this point to an Israeli journalist as they were sitting one afternoon in a Tel Aviv café, and the man shrugged and smiled. "Ah, well, of course, it goes far beyond that. Visitors from the West, including Jews from New York, always seem to have a problem with Israel, and for a somewhat more general reason than I think they may realize. The difficulty, you see, is that the West has always tended to feel more comfortable with Jews as game sufferers, victims. Their affection for the Jews has arisen from their relationship with them as martyrs—plucky martyrs, perhaps, but necessarily martyrs. Without being really conscious of it, Western Jews still collaborate, I think, in this relationship. However, Israel is the end of all that. The Jew is no longer going to be a martyr, plucky or otherwise, for anyone. So now the West doesn't quite know what to do with us. They don't quite know what to make of us. The Jew in Israel has turned out to be a different proposition altogether. . . ."

The New Canaan

AFTER ALMOST A MONTH among the Arabs, he had landed
in Israel in a warm dusk, the plane swooping in off the Mediterranean over a swift unfurling panorama of orchards, plush
fields, lit boulevards—an approach almost like an operatic overture—and he immediately had the peculiar impression, though
only the night before he had been riding with Palestinians down
a road a few yards from its border, that he had actually arrived
on another continent, on the other side of the globe. Unlike the
Cairo airport—which had seemed strangely idle and glum and
half deserted, its quiet abstraction fretted only by the frenzied
sobs of a fellah pleading with a customs inspector, with his
belongings spilled over the floor at his feet—now banked behind
the rail at the Tel Aviv airport this ripe May evening was a
dense thrumming crowd, milling and exultant and expectant,
most of them dressed as if they had arisen only a few minutes
ago from supper tables, from canvas lawn chairs in back yards,
where they had been talking with neighbors over glasses of tea
in the twilight. Watching them, he felt the first brief flush of
a different energy, voltage in the air. Passengers would finally

pass on through customs into enveloping embraces, shouts, bombarding slaps on the back: one father carrying a briefcase just managed to catch his small daughter in one arm as she leapt up to him, while his son, a boy of about twelve wearing short pants, took his other hand and led him on to their mother. It occurred to the American that still nowhere else in the world do air terminals, harbors, ports of arrival have quite the meaning they have here.

Then he was riding through the muggy breaths of the night toward Tel Aviv, under arching yellow lights of an expressway that could have been some southeast Texas turnpike, passing across a grassy flat land littered with high-tension towers and processing plants, a faint murk of sulfur in the air, reaching at last the outskirts of Tel Aviv, vast bulks of apartment buildings like glimmering cliffs in the night, families sitting on balconies with glimpses of blue fluttering television screens through doorways behind them, and the evening sidewalks below them paced by luxurious-legged young girls in taut light shorts. Then, entering Tel Aviv, he found himself in the midst of a gaseous bawling seethe of cars, a snarl and chatter and coughing of countless motor scooters reminiscent more of Rome or Paris than any American city—the streets here filled not with a limitless uproar of voices like Cairo but with the clatter and squall of machinery, a ceaseless gnashing of gears. But after checking into his hotel, he set out for a short walk and presently discovered, tucked off into intricate back streets, a dense neighborhood of stucco apartments snugly huddled in the soundlessly murmuring patterns of leaf shadows, a faint ripple of voices spilling down now and then from overhead balconies, and stray savors of supper, a mild tinkling of glasses, lingering along the intimate sidewalks where, in the shadows under the street lights, occasional strangers passed him with light nods that seemed to him like brief casual wordless blessings. After Egypt, after Jordan, he felt now as if his breath were suddenly released from some long constriction, some dull compression; he already felt loosed into new easy free expanses of the spirit. Turning a corner finally, he came on a bright expansive boulevard of drugstores and supermarkets and bookshops which still remained open for these leisurely evening hours, the sidewalks under the acacia trees surging and eddying with people: countless girls of a spectacularly abundant almost violent lushness, clad in bluejeans and slight sleeveless knit sweaters, swinging with their long loose hair past open-air cafés where students, young soldiers, old men, and solitary spinsterish ladies were sitting at small circular wire-leg tables, reading from books pressed open beside coffee cups and empty sherbert glasses. Now and then, he passed mothers who were actually quietly singing to the children in their arms.

Indeed—unlike Egypt, which had been old beyond his ken— he began to suspect before long in Israel that he was in a totally new order on the face of the earth, a society that was truly something new under the sun, inevitably boggling to all projections and expectations devised from distant references. It seemed implausibly assembled out of an even more ethnically conglomerate collection of peoples than the United States. Along Tel Aviv's endless motley oceanside battery of regal and dowdy hotels, there were certain vagrant mirrorings of Miami and Palm Beach, sidewalk milk bars and glittering art shops and fur salons under the softly clacking plumages of palm trees, with freckled orange-coiffured matrons in rhinestoned butterfly sunglasses and candy-pink smocks snapping along the sidewalks in pink stiletto heels. But haunting the side streets was a population that seemed translated directly out of the murkier recesses of the old Polish and

Russian ghettos: gnomish tattered pushcart peddlers and tallowy ragged-bearded divines in sooty ankle-length topcoats, curb-side hawkers in baggy pin-stripe suits who would step quickly and noiselessly forward at the approach of a stranger and dangle gently chinkling bracelets and necklaces (this haphazard diversity seeming at moments to approach an incoherence, with occasional signs venturing, "Get a Foothold in Israel! —Anglo-Saxon Real Estate Company"); sturdy ample-paunched middle-aged cabdrivers, boomingly convivial, balding under last crispings of hair like gray wire, from Holland or Austria; here and there, in the steam of restaurant kitchens or waiting at bus sheds, dark shy figures, as thin and slight as skinned rabbits, just arrived from Yemen and Libya and still a little uneasy and uncertain after their metamorphosis from turbans and striped gowns into Western clothes; and professors, Heidelberg-educated editors and newspaper columnists who sat in their small back-yard gardens in the blue dusk with pipes and whiskey-sodas talking of Bellow and Mailer and Norman Podhoretz while golden spaniels lounged in the grass by their chairs.

But in this universal eclectic accumulation of peoples, there was nevertheless the air of a measureless family reunion after two thousand years, as if the classic Jewish sense of family had not, as the kibbutzim suggested, been lost in Israel, but had merely amplified to the size of the entire country. As hectically put together as the United States, Israel yet seemed invested with an extra resource, an extra dimension of nationhood that America finally did not have: a general cohesion deriving from that protean circumstance of their common epic experience of Jewishness in exile, a fundamental collective identity arising not out of any real racial unity or the fact of having long abided in a single geographical setting, but out of a shared two-thousand-year historical condition. They know who they are. "The basic ideological concensus in Israel now is probably stronger than it is anywhere else in the world," asserted one Israeli intellectual. "We may indulge in violent interior differences over everything else, but on this question of the rightness and importance of Israel's existence as a nation—there is just no question on that. Perhaps the Arabs believe if they fight the name Zionism, they can defeat us as a state. Well, let there be repudiations of Zionism, Western imperialism, whatever. It doesn't make any difference what happens to names and terms. We don't care what happens to what we are called, to how we are described. Because we are here now, and we *will* exist."

With this final profound intimacy of community despite their disparity, Israel seemed, at the same time, possibly the most rampantly democratic society yet fashioned on the earth—furiously egalitarian, innocent of classes, with even Cabinet ministers returning to their kibbutzim for kitchen duties when their scheduled week arrived. More than his own country, the American thought, there had improbably transpired here on the other side of the globe the kind of nation that would have fulfilled and gladdened the heart of Whitman. For a season last spring, there played in Tel Aviv a somewhat scatological protest play entitled *Queen of the Bath,* a kind of Israeli *MacBird,* which portrayed Defense Minister Moshe Dayan as a zestful murderer and Premier Golda Meir as a nationalistic Valkyrie constantly marveling over the fact that she had never been wrong about anything; Dayan himself had been among those who attended one of its early performances, and his only remark when he emerged afterward from the theatre was a somewhat wistful observation that it would no doubt refresh certain souls in Cairo. Mentioning this, one Israeli editor offered, "You know, despite all the traumatic fears engendered by this long conflict with our neighbors, an extraordinary freedom of awareness and expression has actually been preserved here, both in public debate and our styles of life. While fighting like Sparta, we continue to live the life of Athens. But I must tell you, it has never been here as you might guess from Leon Uris and *Exodus*. I doubt if you'd find many societies so filled with contentiousness, with such a highly argumentative and fractious people. It's quite remarkable, I must say."

In the end, what made Israel seem at least a hemisphere removed from the Arab societies around it—indeed, this was probably the essential complication in the whole thing, that its only correlation with its neighbors was the mere physical happenstance of a mutual geography—was its cultivation of an almost exorbitant individualism, an extravagant personal cherishing of individual existences, whether close to them or unknown. "Of course, we are a fairly compact country, which heightens such an awareness," an Israeli professor explained, "and there is also the fact that when you have been through so much, when you are going through so much now, each life tends to become terribly dear." While the American was eating lunch one afternoon at a modest café in Afula, a farming community in the Jezreel Valley, the portable radio his driver had placed on the table beside their plates began emitting those spaced grave beeps which, introducing newscasts every half hour, momentarily arrest all voices, all motion over the length of Israel; the announcer proceeded to read the names of casualties who had been lost that morning in an ambush along the Lebanese border, and at a nearby table three young soldiers ceased their brawling conversation in midsentence and slowly twirled their bottles of beer between their fingers as they listened, only the faintest flicker of a muscle along their taut jaw lines as each name was pronounced. Gathered at the far end of the room was a party of three men and a woman, and as the radio announcer's voice tolled on, the woman leaned back from the table and crossed her arms, once shaking her head and releasing a long sigh, gazing absently at the floor beside her—in that suddenly hushed and solemn room, they could have been receiving official notification of some actual personal loss, some private disaster.

It seemed one place at least where breath was truly hitting the bottom of the lungs—where human experience was being realized at full spectrum, full octave. To be sure, this he had vaguely expected; as a professor in Jerusalem remarked, "Life almost inevitably is going to be more vibrant under the tension we have known here since 1948, and particularly since 1967." Whatever the causes, he was aware, everywhere around him, of a vivid electric feverishness. (Whenever an Israeli government minister or cabdriver would pause in his conversation and then intone, "I dell you somding—" the phrase somehow carried a special charge of portent; it was no idle rhetorical flourish, the announcement had meaning—something in fact singular and crucial was about to be communicated from one human being to another.) He rode one afternoon from Kiryat Shmona in upper Galilee back down to Tel Aviv in a reeling rickety bus filled with young mothers who were constantly kissing the babies in their laps with loud elaborate smacks, sparrowlike old men in droopy suits who kept compulsively bobbing to their feet to rearrange their string-tied cardboard suitcases on the overhead racks with fierce querulous mutterings, young soldiers with UZIs slung over their backs standing in the door wells and eating half-shucked ears of roasted corn, while the radio speakers overhead played Strauss waltzes and Rimsky-Korsakov's *Sche-*

herazade and, once, even Mendelssohn's Wedding March. It was a small self-contained traveling festival, carried uninterrupted on down out of Galilee's highlands into the Jezreel Valley, the bus lumbering now along a highway like a narrow aisle between endlessly flickering eucalyptus trees, past a honeyed landscape resembling more than anything else California's hot hazed inland vegetable valleys, slim dark ranks of poplars fringing wide fields of avocados, cabbages, gladioli, beets, over which the innumerable plumes of sprinklers played in drowsing myriad shimmers. Occasionally, through the leaves of pear orchards along the road, there was a quick fluttering glimpse of the stumpy remains of an old Crusader fortress. He reached Tel Aviv at sunset, and took a public limousine taxi on to Jerusalem, passing at dusk through the small city of Ramallah, where he peered out his window at a twinkling pageantry of apartment courtyards and delicatessens and libraries and pool halls, the sidewalks under the trees here also swimming with evening strollers, the streets brimming with an infinite jingling of bicycle bells, youths crowded into the curbside cafés relishing from their tables the vagrant passage of girls as profuse and lavish as fireflies. *Maybe they just have a special genius for the twilight hours,* he thought. In full darkness now, he watched the driver with a furtive uneasiness in the panel lights of the limousine—one of that haggard fleet of conveyances called "cheroots" that careen back and forth between Tel Aviv and Jerusalem on through the far hours of the night—snapping his head fitfully from side to side to keep awake, repeatedly swiping half slaps across his stubbled cheeks, smoking successive cigarettes down to glowing red needle points as he carried his passengers, with a lunging hectic unflagging urgency that seemed the common pitch of the whole country, on up the mountain ascents toward Jerusalem.

One afternoon in Jerusalem, he finally attended a session of the Knesset, Israel's parliament—an assembly for the most part of tieless men with the collars of their shirts outside their coat lapels, gathered in the Knesset's modest compact chamber of dark wood paneling with pale grape carpeting and salmon-colored seats, listening now to a speech by Golda Meir. They could have been a collection of labor-union officials or neighborhood grocers meeting in a natty new suburban shopping-center movie theatre, spotlit with the intermission lights, in maybe Phoenix, Arizona. Behind the speaker's rostrum, on a long stark wall of massive granite blocks, there was a single large picture—the blowup of some old dim daguerreotype portrait—of Theodor Herzl, the Zionist patriarch, with the great disguising bramble of beard and dark sunken shadowy eyes of those historical titans out of the second half of the nineteenth century, figures who all tend to register as slightly tainted and suspicious to the American eye, who all inevitably have the look of Marx and Engels—our own political decencies and sanctities, our own patriots, are of the eighteenth century, clean-shaven and pigtailed and somehow more antiseptic.

On the podium beneath Herzl's calm mossy visage, Mrs. Meir was delivering her speech, a major official commentary on those continuing consequences of Herzl's vision accomplished, the long conflict with the Arabs. But in Mrs. Meir's voice was some dry tone, detectable even in Hebrew, of exasperation and brisk reproof, as if she were addressing herself to a problem of simple inveterate cantankerousness on the part of the Arabs—and, indeed, she seemed a woman like an apotheosis of all dour formidable grammar-school principals of one's childhood, her hair pulled back with a tight and faintly frizzled rippling into a bun low on her neck, wearing this afternoon a plain sensible blue suit, a wad of tissue clenched in one hand, as she read on through her speech with ponderous deliberation. ("The only trouble with Golda," whispered a Jerusalem newspaper editor sitting beside the American in the balcony, "is that her Hebrew isn't too good when she tries to make her way through a long text like this.") Her arms folded resolutely on the lectern and her head lowered intently over her script, glasses lodged on her singular imposing nose, she now and then briefly lifted one fore-finger from her crossed arms as if in admonition. Through the entire two hours of her address, there was only a single mild incidental puff of humor, laughter from the floor. Once she propped her forehead momentarily against the fingertips of one hand as if in a fleeting sag of weariness, yet without any pause or lag or alteration in the slow toneless inexorable progression of her voice—and she seemed suddenly to the American like some Tolstoyan figure, like the old Russian general in *War and Peace,* as calm and enduring and patient and implacable as the earth, as weather, as a simple element of nature itself. When she at last finished her speech, she tidily gathered together her papers and, with a slight absent nod toward the applause, dis-mounted from the podium, carefully, in her blunt white ox-fords, her plump ankles filmed in white cotton stockings, her head drooping forward, seeming suddenly enormously alone: having been named Prime Minister after the death of Levi Eshkol as a kind of compromise interval custodian to avoid a major disruptive clash between certain more conspicuous gov-ernment personalities, she had emerged since then as one of that company of leaders, like Pope John, who, initially sup-posed to be transitory occurrences, turn out—perhaps because of a freedom from any special expectations for them—to be monu-mental figures. Making her way on to her seat at the front row of the chamber, she sat there motionless for a few moments and then, unobtrusively, slipped her white purse out from under her desk lid, merely holding it in her ample lap for a few moments longer, her two hands lying over the snap and her feet planted wide apart, glancing idly around her. "Look at her now," the editor whispered to the American. "She wants to take a smoke, but they won't let you smoke in here, so she'll just wait a few minutes and then get up and slip out in the hall to light up. . . ." And presently she unsnapped her purse, reached in it briefly with one hand plunged in past her wrist, and finally brought up a package of Chesterfields, which she held just for an instant not quite out of the purse while she delicately withdrew a cigarette, clicking the purse shut then and shoving it back under her desk. But for several more minutes, she merely dandled the unlit cigarette in her fingers while she looked casually around her, once or twice nodding to a legislator. Then, with Dayan on the podium delivering a report, she finally quietly arose and plodded slowly on up the aisle, out of the chamber.

Actually, back in the United States before his departure, the journalist had discovered that the romance about Israel, after twenty years, was rapidly withering in some quarters—a disenchantment probably beginning after 1967, when Israel's almost effortless rout of the Arab armies introduced, at the least, considerable complications into the old image of a doughty spindly David trying to hold off a baleful Goliath. He had found an impatient cynicism, a slight frostiness, had begun to infiltrate certain ruminations about Israel in New York intellectual caverns and New Left campus seminars: in particular, the reflection that Israel was actually founded on an atrociously reactionary premise, as an ethnic nation, ethnically exclusive. "After all,

look at the whole thing now," insisted one member of Manhattan's literati; "it has got to be the most atavistic nation on
earth, hasn't it? It's a throwback to the nineteenth century. I
mean the very idea of anybody, in this time, trying to set up a
Volksland. . . ."

Indeed, from afar, it was a perspective, a judgment, that ac-
quired some plausibility. By all the abstract political proprieties,
Israel did seem inarguably gauche—nationalistic, militaristic,
not to mention racist. But once in Israel itself, he discovered that,
experientially, Israel was altogether as impossible an event to
contain with political analysis, abstractions, ideological definitions as the whole long saga of the Jews' survival as a people.
It answered all the speculations about it from afar, but they did
not comprehend it. In the end, it seemed to amount to nothing
less than an enigma, beyond the formal symmetries and circum-
scriptions of political and ideological definitions. "We actually
have no precedents, no perspectives for ourselves and our problems," asserted an Israeli writer. "Right from the beginning, we
have had to ad-lib the whole thing." In fact, it was as if Israel's
peculiar genius, as a human society, was that its governmental
system and social structures existed only as incidental makeshift
conveniences, mere expediencies which did not really describe
it, while it actually answered to some simple formless unpre-
meditated instinct for life beyond any formulation, worked
closer than any other society to the final limitless mystery of
human existence—to its perplexity, its paradoxes of the earthly
and the soulful, its sheer deep disordered energies. Though it
has been physically realized, Israel—even more fully than the
Palestinian phenomenon—amounts to an existential nation, a
not mediocre occurrence in history: the advent of a society that
approximates a collective continual poem, whose unarticulated
constitution is a lyric sense of life.

Even so, it is possible that, as it took forty years in the wilderness for a true Hebraic folk to emerge from Moses's ragtag stampede of refugees, only now—with the generation just cresting—is Israel reaching its final accomplishment. The driver of one cab that the journalist flagged in Tel Aviv was a burnt burnished sandaled youth with rumpled black locks who jubilantly announced, "No, no, not speak English. Not speak French, not speak Italian. English for England, America. French for France. But I—I am Israeli. I speak only Hebrew. . . ." A professor in Jerusalem, sitting in the study of his home one afternoon with the American journalist, proposed that "the youth around us now are not nearly so vocal about things as my own generation— no doubt, they got so spoon-fed on ideology when they were children it finally turned their stomach. The other day I picked up a young soldier hitchhiking on the road, and when I asked him if he was committed to the army as a career, he said, 'What, are you crazy? You think I am army-sick?' But while they would never use our phraseology, they are actually more committed to Israel, I believe, than we were. Probably 1967 enhanced their feeling, their very intense feeling, of belonging here in their own creation. During those crisis days of 1967, it seemed they finally became *personally* aware of what happened during the holocaust in Germany, and with that crisis Israel became for them not something ideological but truly concrete and heroic. It is a feeling, of course, that deepens as the crisis continues. It is not so much a religious thing, but a sense for them of a long historical and cultural continuity. Like my son—whatever he reads in the Bible is here; the circle is closed for him. I don't know, maybe it's some inherited memory of homelessness, but their instinct for the ancient landscapes, for going into the desert, is something like I've never seen before. The truth is, existentially, they are *super*patriots. . . ." Toward the end of the conversation, the professor's daughter entered the room to ask him something in Hebrew—a tall girl, trim and blond and lithe as an antelope, wearing jeans and a man's khaki shirt, with a remote, serene, almost graven composure about her, glancing only briefly at the visitor—and when she left the room, her father turned to the American and murmured, with a small faltering smile, "Her fiancé, you know, two weeks ago—he was killed on the Canal. . . ."

A few days later, in a hushed early morning just after dawn as he was waiting in the empty lobby of his hotel to be driven to a base near the Canal, the bell captain—a stout freckled youth who looked to be no more than eighteen—informed him with a wide grin, "I go next week to Canal also. Third time for me, yes. But I volunteer. Is very hard life there, but all my friends at the Canal. I like it better there, yes, than here. So I go back next week, I be with them again." Actually, all Israeli boys, the American learned, are required to serve three years of military duty (two for girls) right after graduation from high school, before they enter college—"which makes," suggested one university administrator, "for a somewhat soberer population on our campuses. They have seen something of life before they arrive here." But riding once along the Lebanese border, he came on a young corporal strolling along the road with his girl; she had come up from Jerusalem to spend this Sunday afternoon with him, and after chatting briefly with the American, the two of them proceeded on down the road to a guard tower where, only a matter of yards from the Lebanese border, the young corporal climbed up and demonstrated for her how the turret ingeniously turned in all directions, energetically cranking it slowly around while she watched him from below, smiling brightly and raptly. Indeed, for all its legendary deadly precision, the Israeli army, from the youths at the front to its somewhat rumpled officers at headquarters, still seemed to have the informal quality of a guerrilla force about it, existing in a casual and easy cohabitation with civilian society.

After his driver picked him up at the hotel that morning, they headed down the coastal Plain of Ashkelon toward the Canal—past a meticulously and intricately tilled countryside like Missouri or Iowa farm land contracted to a Lilliputian scale, one placid green field supposedly the site where Samson had loosed the torch-tailed foxes among the Philistines' corn after their mischief at his wedding feast. Crossing then out of the pre-1967 boundary of Israel into the territory taken in the Six-Day War, it was as if they had passed instantly back four thousand years into the very genesis of the Jews themselves: trailing across the wastes of the sand around them were occasional solitary processions of Bedouins, a dark tattered wild people like lingering phantom images of the Hebrews themselves just straggled out of Egypt—"There's no doubt our Mosaic ancestors lived just like these people," his driver observed, "would, in fact, be indistinguishable from these people. Every time we come out here, it's like looking at ourselves four thousand years ago. This is even the general area, up here in the northern part of the Sinai, where a lot of scholars now maintain the Israelites passed those forty years in the wilderness after they escaped Egypt, before they moved on to the Jordan. . . ." (Prior to entering the occupied territory, his driver had stopped at a filling station café, and as they were sipping coffee at the counter, there was a sudden battering howl of jets passing overhead, annihilating for an instant all other sound; everyone in the café immediately arose and scrambled outside in the yard to watch the planes skimming on off into the distance, toward the front—a reaction, actually, he had noticed before in Israel, in restaurants and shops out beyond the cities, whenever there was a rush of jets overhead: a constant furious vigilance toward any sounds or appearances in the sky, as if it were still up there above them that all mortal affairs and destinies on the ground were ultimately being determined and negotiated, as in the ancient stagecraft of the gods.)

Approaching the Canal on a narrow road like a single trivial flimsy tape of pavement dwindling off across the limitless indifferent face of the desert, they passed now and then an army water truck barging along with its cab windows rolled down, its radio blaring "Love Is Blue," brief bawling gusts of Diana Ross and the Supremes. At last they reached the base where the American was to await final clearance to go on to the Canal—a collection of Quonset huts, quiet and musing in the morning, surrounded by dunes from which there bristled anti-aircraft guns. But there were only intermittent low grumblings to the east, in the bare blue sky, and a soldier somewhere nearby was singing to himself, his voice trailing thinly over the sunny compound, "Ai-yai, yai-yai . . . Come to my *win*-dow. . . ." The American was taken on to one of the Quonset huts, shown into a low cramped room where he found a noisy churning nest of people, young soldiers and girls, with airline travel posters of Los Angeles's scintillant twilight hills, Paris's filigreed streets, as well as photographs of the Wailing Wall and Absalom's Tomb, tacked over the plywood and tin sheeting around them. Somehow he had the sensation, watching the ceaseless wash of people and voices in and out of the door, that he was sitting in a college dormitory room on the Saturday morning before the Homecoming game. The base administrator himself could have been the center for some small campus football squad, a burly youth, a bit untidy and drowsy as if he had just awakened from a nap, with uncombed sandy hair and an open affable simple face, but casually confident, constantly flipping a key chain in his fingers. He sat most of the time, one leg heavily plopped across the corner of his desk, in a spectacularly flamboyant chair, round-backed and upholstered in burnt-orange velvet, with the faintly decadent gorgeousness of a curio lifted out of some Casablanca bordello parlor: asked about it, the youth grinned a bit sheepishly, slapping one of its armrests, and said, "Yes, the Egyptian commander at this base, he left it behind in his hurried departure in 1967. We have been holding it for him, but it seems he hasn't come back yet to pick it up."

Presently, two officers entered the room—rabbis, one of them with a full black Mosaic beard—with a girl following behind them carrying a typewriter, which she placed on an oilcloth-covered table by a window, shoving aside a rifle. The two rabbis took the chairs that were quickly offered them, the bearded one leaning back against the wall, silent, expressionless, his eyes strangely remote and dull, while he watched the other one, sitting now behind the desk in the Egyptian commander's chair, trying to place a call through the wall phone beside him, a man with a fresh bland genial face and thinning vague hair, but his manner now delicately harried and effusive with the suggestion of a fine fraying. Then a young corporal leaned toward the American and muttered, "They have been here since yesterday afternoon. Thirteen of our soldiers were killed yesterday along the Canal in an Egyptian ambush, but the bombing has been too heavy for them to get to the bodies. So they have been waiting since yesterday for it to lift, without any sleep. That is why you are having to wait also, because the planes—" The American stared at the corporal: "You mean thirteen soldiers from *this* base, from right here?" "Yes, from here," said the corporal, and the American said, "You mean you knew some of them? Everybody in here knew them?" The corporal nodded, "Yes, of course. It is very tragic. Everyone is trying not to show how they feel about it now. But we knew them, yes. They were our friends. . . ." The girl at the table by the window was now clattering out a report on the typewriter, her face vacant, blowing back a strand of hair now and then from her cheek, pausing only once to wipe the back of her wrist across her forehead. The chaplain behind the desk finally gave the phone to someone else to try to establish a better connection, and then turned to the American and began constructing small pleasantries, a cordial smile fixed on his face. Then, at a soft call from behind him, he abruptly swirled around and snatched the phone again, shouting into the receiver the names of the dead—bellowing each name again and again, as if even this last trace of their realities, their names, were already dimming into an obliteration of static on an uncertain connection.

Here the American waited through the day, on into the late hours of the afternoon, escorted once to the officers' mess, for lunch, where the subdued clamor of voices and clinking of tableware at one point abruptly vanished in a tremendous shriek of jets—those celestial machines of their fate—blasting past low overhead, blowing the curtains inward over the tables. For all that, the idle cheerful swarming continued in the room, girls materializing from outside to lounge for a while on the edge of the table by the window in their khaki blouses and skirts, sleek and rippling as otters, with smoky tans, exchanging light laughs and cuffs on the shoulder with the youths around them. Among them was one dark opulent girl, who listened to the banter with little soundless laughs, as if she were partaking lusciously of some constant glee and exhilaration in bright eager glistening bites, and finally a tall and leonine young sergeant, as he left the room, reached over and briefly muffed her hair, and she made a swipe for his hand as he went out the door.

At last he was taken to the Canal, clumping in helmet and flak vest down a lightless tunnel into a bunker where a young officer, sleeping on an elevated cot with his arms wrapped around his shoulders, his back to the burning light bulb, began stirring at the sound of voices mumbling below him. After peering a moment over his shoulder at the strangers there, he slowly heaved himself down to a lower bunk where he sat for a while longer, blinking, rubbing his face with both hands: there was a kind of Persian glamour to his features, with luminous black eyes and dark extravagant eyebrows, and finally he murmured, his voice still sluggish and full of sleep, "No, nothing is hard, nothing is hard. Is better that we are sitting on the Canal than the Egyptians should be sitting in Tel Aviv. We are appreciating the Egyptian soldier, of course, but we are not afraid of him. When our planes were bombing and the Egyptians weren't answering, that made us feel good. But even with the Egyptians bombing now, that is not the end of the world. Our spirits are high. . . ." He then said something in Hebrew to the lieutenant who had brought the American there, his eyes briefly flaring wide, and the lieutenant muttered to the American, "Well, perhaps, if you are finished, maybe we go now. . . ."

On the way back to the base, after they had passed a guard post, the lieutenant—pale and bespectacled and frail under his bulky helmet—began shedding his gear, his helmet and his flak vest, and yelled to the American over the noise of the jeep, "You see, when we leave the front, when we pass the point, we relax. We take off the war with our equipment. We know everything is normal again." When they reached the base again, they were greeted as they climbed out of the jeep by a pert and twinkling girl with a short-cropped thatch of jet-black hair, wearing lavender slacks and a flowered blouse—a student at Hebrew University in Jerusalem who had come out with her notes and textbooks to spend the day with the lieutenant—and the American watched the two of them walking off across the sandy yard between the Quonset huts, the little fingers of their hands loosely latched, softly clinging, while at the other end of the yard the chaplains now were clambering aboard separate waiting jeeps, holding small black satchels against their chests.

When he got back to Jerusalem, the American took a cab after dinner to Hebrew University, getting out in the high cool night to find the campus still milling with students under a general flare of lights, youths surging with a glad uproar everywhere over the sweet grass of evening. Lost among them, the American wandered into a student center, a long low room that was crowded with that violent smoky impact of a Saturday-night cockfight, where—on two tables in the center of the room, in the foggy glare of a spotlight—a boy and a girl were dancing in dreaming luxurious throes like some ecstatic rite, some unscriptured tribal celebration of life from their ancient odyssey in the desert, some ghost of Judith's dance after their arrival into the Land of Canaan. The American thought as he made his way back outside, *They are still living not only in Isaiah and Gideon and Amos; they are also still living in that other portion of their soul, as deep and enduring: the Song of Solomon.* . . .

But the kibbutzim still constitute, in a sense, the quick, the essence of Israel. Although they now account for only some four percent of the nation's population, they provide an inordinate

proportion of Israel's military and governmental leaders, form-
ing a kind of national farming gentry, a hardy rural élite
detached from the complex urbanities of the cities. But most
of them, after twenty years, have mellowed somewhat as
frontier outposts, more resembling—with guest houses now
and lobbies with postcard racks and souvenir shops—sedate
tourist retreats. The American stayed overnight in one kibbutz
called Kfar Blum in upper Galilee, near the Lebanese border,
which was originally settled in the forties by expatriate American
Jews. Arriving on a Sunday afternoon, he found youths playing
soccer in bathing suits on a grassy lawn beside a swimming pool,
and after registering he walked over the grounds until supper-
time. The last soft sunlight of the afternoon was lingering in
the tops of fir trees with a far chortling and hooting of doves,
swallows pinwheeling across the pale evening sky; in the neat
mown yards of low shallow houses, under mimosa trees and
cedars and pear trees, there was a dim green gloom like light
in an aquarium, with bicycles occasionally flickering noiselessly
past on the walkways, mothers pushing children in strollers, the
sound of a child's sudden gleeful cackling coming from one
screened back porch—an hour, a quiet, filled with the simple
small noises of a day's calm completion. At dinner, a large
assemblage of tourists from England sat at a long table near him,
wearing Bermuda shorts and yarmulkes, and singing Jewish
hymns. The plump aproned woman who was waiting on tables
that evening brought the American a salad, and when he de-
clined it, she lifted her eyebrows, "So—you're so healthy, you
don't need the vitamins? . . ." But the next morning, standing
with the kibbutz leader along a dirt road waiting for a bus to
take him back to Tel Aviv, with wide groomed fields of vegetables yawning around him, he could hear distant dull slams of

artillery from the mountains, and the kibbutz leader began re-
miniscing with a woman who was waiting with another party
of visitors about the days in 1948, when they were fighting in
those mountains: "Twenty years—but, listen: it's still just as
close to us. . . ."

Even closer to that mortal line that has lasted since 1948 is
Kfar Rupin, a kibbutz whose lights, that night just a week
before with the Palestinians, he had seen glimmering from the
other side of the Jordan. When he visited it one bright afternoon, he found, beneath date palms and eucalyptus trees swimming in a hot wind, walkways with ruffles of petunias that led
to bunkers. Here, since 1967, the children of Kfar Rupin have
been sleeping, the stairs descending past walls decorated with an
almost desperate festiveness, daubed with gaudy purple birds
and orange peacocks and red sunbursts, and in the rooms below,
with their ranks of children's bunks bolted to the walls, small
ventilation fans had been discreetly installed near the ceiling.
The kibbutz leader, a man who introduced himself as Czech,
explained, "Yes, we are building in all the bunkers now anti-gas
facilities. The Arabs, they used gas in Yemen against each
other—we should think they would not use it against us?" He
shrugged. "But you see, we try to make the shelters friendly
places, because the youngest children here—those born after
1967—they have never spent a night aboveground. But I heard
the children talking the other day; one of them was wondering
why we always show the bunkers to visitors, and another one said,
'Because they are poor people who do not have shelters where
they come from.' . . ." Czech himself could have been a walking,
breathing incarnate symbol of Israel: a stumpy and gristled
figure, bowlegged, hefty as a fireplug, with a blunt battered
durable face, he had passed through the cataclysm in Europe

during the forties and then fought in the 1948 war against the Arabs; there dwelt in him a great gusto for ballet, an exquisite shrewdness in gardening despite his stubby grimed mechanic's fingers, and he was given through the course of that afternoon to repeated effusions about the birds they passed, in a voice that sounded like a rake scraping across pavement: "Look! See there—kingfisher! Ah, very nice bird. . . ." With a huge flecked smoke-gray mastiff constantly floating along behind him, he walked with a slight lurching limp left from a fall during an archaeological climb some years ago in the desert, taking the American to the kibbutz's cultural center, a modern stucco structure which, he reported, had been shelled a few nights before while a ballet was under way: "The dancer, she fell down when the first shell hit, you know. But right away, she got back up, the ballet went on. Now tonight here, we have cinema. Tomorrow, a wedding . . ." Once, as he was driving the American to show him the fields, the jeep passed a power station which gave a sudden throbbing whine, and Czech instantly flinched back, ducking his head, the jeep momentarily veering, but with only the slightest pause in his ebullient booming discourse: "We never stop our cultural life; we never shutting the lights. If we stop our work, they are winning—" Indeed, it was like a dogged furious rampant cultivation of life right up to the very fringe of death, with terraced layers of fishponds extending on through barbed wire and sentry towers to the twining edge of the Jordan, beet fields diligently tilled among trenches and concrete pillboxes by tractors with armored underplating as a protection against mines. "We are not heroes," Czech declared in a husking croak. "We are normal people. Everyone is afraid, sure. There are some old people here, every night at six o'clock they want to go down in the bunker to watch TV. They stay down there all through the evening, three, four hours, just sitting there watching TV. All right, I tell them, so be afraid—watch TV in the bunkers every evening, is all right. But don't leave. Just don't leave. Because if you leave, they are winning."

Something Tragic in the Air

IN THIS RESPECT more than any other, kibbutzim like Kfar Rupin remain emblems of all Israel: for twenty years, they have been dwelling at the actual physical edge of extinction. Israel, of course, was conceived in the holocaust, issued directly out of Dachau and Buchenwald—that single greatest crime in the memory of man, the Eating of the Apple for the whole race, so that now we have glimpsed the darker territories of our common nature. At the same time, this spiritual apprehension in Europe coincided with that other cosmic nibble in the Pacific; Nagasaki and Hiroshima were in a way a technological counterpart, the apprehension of a means, a machinery, for evil of corresponding magnitude—the moral perception in Europe providing perhaps just enough pause to insure against that machinery being used, at least for a while.

The passage of the Jews through the holocaust has become as definitive and protean an event now of Jewish history as the Passover Night in Egypt over three thousand years ago. It is, actually, a lasting trauma in which Israel still lives, and which continues, in a way, to sustain it: the dark maw of Auschwitz still looms immediately at its back; the lights of the kibbutzim along the Jordan are also, in a sense, still glimmering against that old mad midnight in the forties. The American spent one evening with the family of a kibbutz leader in upper Galilee, sitting in a small plain living room and chatting over glasses of sweet-breathed Israeli brandy, with an undertone of grave music, the singing of a Gregorian choir, playing from another room: at one point, the kibbutz leader—a quiet chunky balding man who had immigrated from America during the forties— proposed in an even mild voice, with a steady whimsical smile, "You see, for over four thousand years somebody or other has been trying to destroy us. Now we're faced with the threat again, this time with help from the Russians. Well, I moved here from the States because I decided that if I was going to die, it would at least be in my own land. And we cannot lose here, because it would be Buchenwald again—only, this time it would be the end. If we lose here now, we lose forever."

Indeed, conceived in such a desperation, having existed more or less in that same desperation ever since, Israel even contains some people who are given to uneasy speculations about what would actually befall the nation if the compressions of that imminence of extinction were removed. But at the same time, there are deeper misgivings now about whether any society, any nation, can live for very long, much less twenty-two years, from such a reference point, a single premise where everything comes finally to a matter of annihilation or survival, without the exigencies and tensions accompanying such a proposition beginning at last to work certain quiet erosions, constrictions, disfigurements on that nation's mind and spirit. "In fact, this is what I would call the real menace, beyond ordnance ratios, that is posed by the Arabs," allowed one Israeli intellectual. "The danger is what might happen to us in fortifying ourself against Arab aggression. If this were deliberate, it would be a piece of exquisite cunning on the part of the Arabs. . . ." Actually, the American came across intimations that, in its long fortress existence, a certain Cold War mentality had begun emerging in Israel reminiscent of the psychology in the United States during the early fifties; not only did there seem a disposition toward Dulles-like visions of Russia's monolithic malevolence but also there was dismay among some Israeli liberals about a growing pinch on debate and dialogue within the country. A major Israeli writer, who was later dismissed with a brittle laugh by a Jerusalem newspaper editor as "our comic dove," glumly declared in his Tel Aviv apartment one evening, "It is beginning now in the country that if you talk about giving back territory at all, about any concessions whatsoever to the Arabs, you are going to be called a traitor. There is beginning here a kind of McCarthyism, I'm afraid. And the people most worried about this, you will find, are the armed forces—they know that when people start calling other people traitors in the course of debate about policies, that means they have started setting up their own private patriotism, you see, and that kind of thing is going to cause a nation to disintegrate sooner or later. This is something that is beginning to worry the army very much." The popular outlook toward the Arabs, what's more, tends to evoke what has been that lingering chill shade left in America's thinking from the Cold War mentality, the rationale for Vietnam: "They tell us to withdraw," one cabdriver offered. "What, they want us to fight them outside Tel Aviv? Better it should be in the desert. If you're not going to do it proper, there's only one thing that remains—the Mediterranean." One foreign-ministry official, commenting on Israel's appearance of diplomatic implacability, explained, "The thing you must understand is that if we are generous now, it would be interpreted by the Arabs as a sign of weakness."

Somehow, though, there seemed to be even more disquieting resonances, left from the 1967 war, at play at the edges of Israel's perspectives now. With a vast hostage population in the occupied territories after its victory, Israel for a while answered incidents of sabotage with a tactic they called "environmental punishment"—demolition operations on the immediate neighborhoods around suspected terrorists' refuges—an expedient they shortly abandoned after the mild clamor it provoked internationally, and which they now tend to discount as merely "an unlucky phrase." But they pursued for some time longer, until Russia's introduction of missile barricades, a policy of bombing raids deep into the interior of Egypt, dusting up to the very suburbs of Cairo: a military spokesman in Jerusalem explained, "We simply wanted to talk directly that way to the Arab people. Nasser and his colleagues had claimed they had destroyed much of the Israeli air force, so we wanted to destroy any illusions they might have about this by hitting and bombing freely their military installations, bombing right up to the edge of Cairo. But really, with continuous deep-penetration raids, we thought that perhaps some sort of pressure would build up from under, from the populace, to force a change in leadership, or at least a change in their intransigence." In the first place, one does not really speak to the Arab sense of reality through the language of pragmatic necessity. Beyond that, the device of persistent and systematic bombing of a country has never proved spectacularly successful in imparting a mood of hopelessness or compliance to those people on the ground being bombed, whether in Britain at the beginning of

World War II, Germany at the end, or twenty years later in North Vietnam. Rather, it usually has something of a reverse effect. What is considerably more puzzling, though, is that Israel, after the devastations of its people in World War II and its ordeal of physical peril since then, could have presumed the efficacy of force toward intimidating a population; for some reason, it seemed possibly the last nation in the world that would make such an assumption about the working of the human spirit. Asked about this, one Israeli leader said somewhat plaintively, "Well, certainly, if there's one policy that hasn't worked against the Arabs, I suppose, it is force. But, then, tell me another. . . ." But a foreign-ministry spokesman proposed, "It just seems there's no way to deal with them except through shocks. The first shock was 1948. Then it took another one in 1956, and then another in 1967. But now it looks like what is needed is yet another shock. I don't necessarily mean a war, maybe just a domestic shock of economic or political crisis inside these countries themselves. Or—yes, another war. But it's going to take a fourth shock somehow to finally bring them around."

Not incidentally, it was no less astonishing that they could have entered into such an estrangement from the simple nature of the human heart, not to mention the eccentricities of the Arab mind, that they could wistfully insist in army offices and government ministries, "The problem of the refugees themselves is really an economic problem. We have proved that on the West Bank, where, as the economic conditions of the Arabs have improved, our difficulties with them have dwindled. Up until 1967, these people in the occupied territories had been living in the Middle Ages, but in Gaza alone now, from only three thousand people using electricity, we now have twenty thousand using it. After all, if you live in a primitive society where no one takes care of your needs, why not fight? What's to lose? This is the problem, same with all the Arab world. They ought to understand that we only want to cross their borders with tractors, not tanks." An army spokesman in Tel Aviv maintained, "What really created the Palestinian problem was the 1967 United Nations resolution—it introduced this different side element of the situation to a political level again, and the Arab states quickly blew it up into a major issue. These commandos—I tell you, we have captured among them Kuwaitis, Algerians, all the riffraff of the world. It's simply something to needle Israel, that's all."

Most improbably now, with a program already quietly under way to transfer a heavy proportion of Palestinians from their weltering and unmanageable concentration in Gaza over into the more scantily inhabited regions of the West Bank, Israel's policies since 1967 have tended to entail massive calculated geopolitical rearrangements; they have begun talking, analyzing the conflict, fashioning approaches for the future in terms of presiding over or at least negotiating redistributions and reconditionings of whole populations, designing new maps. "We have had certain Palestinian groups come to us," reported one foreign-ministry official, "and what we have told them is —who do you actually represent? We can't talk to just any Peter, George, and Jake. If you're really conscious of yourselves now as a nation, as a people—get a capital! Come to us as the government in Amman, then we can talk. Because after all, you know, the Palestinians are already sixty percent of the population over there. . . ." As for their frustrations in assimilating the Arabs in the occupied areas even on a tentative basis, one government spokesman said .with a sigh, "They realize that our system is better than the system they were living under before; they know democracy is a good thing—but they don't know how to digest it. It's like a child trying to become independent of his mother's milk. In whatever territories we retain in the end, it's going to take a long time with the Arab citizens, and it's going to take patience."

Before long, in fact, it seemed to the American he had begun to detect, beyond the lyricism and rampant glee for life, something elusively tragic lurking in the psychic weather of the country. The editor of one Israeli newspaper mused, "You know, there's really no way to measure the deep demoralization that all those centuries of scorn have left in the Jews. You can't go through all that for so many years without it really doing something to you. And Hitler—Hitler really got to them, in ways you couldn't imagine. Beyond the concentration camps and everything, he really got under their skin. But what has happened is that this profound demoralization has taken two forms: one, a general personal mood of defeatism in individuals; and, two, a kind of ferocious public assertiveness, combativeness, that comes really from a general instinctive suspiciousness of everybody around them." It was as if, twenty years after the atrocities visited on them by the Third Reich, now in the homeland that had its inception in those atrocities, they continued to live in aggrievement, in abiding outrage and a sense of embattled isolation, a wounded people who still cultivate a memory of the pain—not unlike, in fact, the mind of the Germans in their destitution after the Versailles Treaty.

The American's contemplation was that when he got back to the States, he would write it, *Some have caught hints. . . .*

There are those who indicate . . . out of some deep aversion
to partaking himself in such ruminations. One of the secret
incidental enterprises in which he had always been earnestly
engaged in his work, he realized, was trying to compensate for
the circumstance—trying to write himself above the fact—that
he happened to be in the second half of the twentieth century,
a white goy Southerner: an unfashionable genus at the moment,
to say the least. As a result, he had diligently practiced in print
a certain moral fastidiousness, always wary of unwittingly
ambushing himself in some lapse into moral inelegance. He
found his suspicions about Israel, then, afforded considerable
discomfort, brought with them a vague queasiness. So he would
write it, *According to some observers,* approach it in that gingerly and genteel fashion. But in his personal broodings he became progressively more dismal: he felt there was something
unsettlingly familiar about the national demeanor. Delivered
out of the holocaust, having survived the scourge, but still
involved in the trauma of what had happened to them twenty-
five years ago, it seemed they had assumed something of the
manner of procedure that was employed in wreaking such
enormous destruction among them, as if that were the only
way to insure against its ever happening to them again—as
often, in horrors like the Nazis' finally inexplicable crime
against the Jews, do the abused come to resemble the abuser,
the brutalized put on the mask of their brutalizers. Whatever,
he could not escape an uneasiness that the crime had left some
ghost, some pattern of itself, in the victim; sitting one morning
in the office of an Israeli foreign-ministry official—a small
plump amiable man with a shiny onion-dome head, wearing a
crisp starched pin-striped shirt, the casement window of the
meager room opened behind him to a dense garden brimming

riotously in the sweet spring morning—he felt some peculiar almost heartbreaking poignancy when the official said, "Why, I even give my shirts to an Arab laundry; I leave my shoes in an Arab shop," then abruptly leaned back and, softly tapping his spread fingertips together, cordially proposed, "Ah, we have maybe a cup of coffee; then we feel better while we talk. . . ."

In particular, Moshe Dayan—who was actually in Palestine during the agonies of Israel's genesis in the waning lurid phantasmagorias of the Third Reich—nevertheless struck the American, with his glazed emaciated face shrunken like a caul close to his skull, some odd uneasy glee in his one eye and shriveled mouth, as an almost melodramatic invocation of both a concentration-camp commander and survivor. "Oh, but that is not fair," declared an Israeli journalist to whom he admitted this haunting. "You must realize that the war has taken a terrible toll on the man—he has been living with it day after day now for three years. He is only very weary."

Indeed, it came to him later that the real melancholy about Israel might lie simply in the fact that the world has always, for some reason, expected more of the Jews than the rest of the human race. Especially, it seemed they had been consecrated and exalted, somehow, by their ordeal in the holocaust; it has supposedly left them, in Israel, with a special tragic wisdom and virtue apart from the incorrigibly venal and brutish manner in which all other nations pursued their interests. The unique lot, the peculiar burden, of Israel was that it had to proceed under this special moral regard and scrutiny from the rest of mankind. But then, of course, such expectations probably came from an old submerged Christian theodramatics still at work, the imposition on them of the role of sufferers for all mankind, by some mystical process redeeming Christendom—along with themselves again for a time—by letting the transgressions and guilt and contrition and conscience of the West act and play over them, enact through them—so that, in this sense, Jesus is not really a Christian symbol: he has always been profoundly a Jewish symbol. But however grotesque the notion, the expectation still seems to linger: a need to believe in the Jews in the old sense, as a people indeed chosen for a special holiness through suffering, and the disappointments with Israel, as the journalist in Tel Aviv had indicated, may merely be a discomfort, a disconcertion, that the Jews seem suddenly to be abjuring this role. It is up to us now to perform our moral dramas on ourselves—they are having no part of it any longer.

It seemed fair to suggest that their victory in 1967, if it was not perversely turning into tragedy for them, at least had led them into certain moral complications. The American sat one afternoon in Jerusalem with an Israeli professor and a Cabinet minister—two old friends who had been conducting these afternoon dialogues over coffee and cigarettes, in this cool tiled room walled with books and with the lattice windows open to soft yellow ripening light in the leaves outside, through many seasons of crisis and dismay and hope, both of them now with sons serving at the front. "Let me say this," ventured the Cabinet minister. "The question comes to what kind of Israel do we want. Territory problems, we don't have: we can fulfill Israel inside the pre-'67 boundaries. For that, we don't need more territories. Listen, the land we don't need; what we need is a change of mind among the Arabs. What we have are security problems. But in a single state, like they're talking, one of us will be the minority, which neither of us will accept. The Jews were slaves along the Nile, why do we want that again? . . ." The professor interposed, "Actually, when it comes to the immediate war aim of security, there are no hawks and doves in Israel. Where the division comes is over what we'll do with the territory. Some want even more, true, out of historical ideology—the manifest destiny. Others want to hold what we have for security. But still others think any objective basis for peace cannot lie in territorial claims of any kind, but has to lie in the Security Council's resolution. In the end, the idea that Israel should rule a big minority of Arabs—this is destructive, I believe; it negates completely the Zionist principle for the self-determination of persecuted minorities."

But with the protraction of the occupation, there has begun to accumulate a deep cynicism in Israel about what one can expect of the Arabs, facilitated by what seems a curiously fitful understanding of the Arab psychology—specifically a tendency to take Arab fulminations with scrupulous literalness, for what they would mean if they were uttered in Tel Aviv or Jerusalem. As one Israeli political scholar pointed out, "You can't imagine how much the population here wants peace. We would concede almost all the territories taken in 1967; we are ready to negotiate with no strings attached. If they want to have their machismo, O.K. If they want to be guerrillas—all right: guerrillas with their machismo intact, so let them now come to talk to us as men to men for mutual guarantees. There is a popular readiness to offer the West Bank, the Gaza Strip, with maybe even a corridor between the two, to repatriate or compensate Palestinians for lands lost in '48, maybe even to set up Jerusalem as an international city, the capital of the U.N. There's a popular willingness for all of this, believe me.

But also, the consensus is, we won't budge an inch until peace is assured. And most people at the moment feel very little alternative, I'm afraid, to holding the cease-fire lines." The difficulty, asserts one Israeli journalist, is that "in the Middle East yesterday's options and crossroads are notorious for getting quickly covered over with sand. For instance, there may have once been easy agreement on the return of Sharm el Sheikh, but it would be quite a stubborn matter today. The more time goes by, the higher the price becomes, the more expensive the stakes. What this is leading to is an attitude that the conflict simply cannot be solved by articulation, by bright little formulas —that what you have is two completely irreconcilable forces caught in a classic Greek tragedy, clashing over irreconcilable interests and therefore determined to destroy each other."

The result is that the protraction of the occupation inevitably fortifies the pessimism, which acts in turn to prolong the conflict, an impasse which then has the effect of protracting the occupation. The point of the misgivings of some Israelis now about this extended inconclusive proprietorship over Arab territories is whether any people can indefinitely preside over another defeated and occupied people without that occupation beginning to work subtle corruptions on the occupiers, damaging in essential moral respects the whole life of the country. Indeed, there are indications that Israel's long occupation of the territories taken in 1967, however accidental an outcome in the beginning, has in itself begun to induce certain acquisitory appetites and tantalizations, a reluctance to relinquish the land for its own sake. One Israeli writer—a small shambling doleful round-eyed panda of a man named Amos Kenan, advertised to the American earlier as "our own Norman Mailer"—observed morosely in the late hours of an evening in Tel Aviv, "To put it bluntly, the Israeli government has managed to intoxicate itself that the Arabs don't want peace at any price. Why? Because they're beginning to discover that they actually don't want to give up the territory after all. So their pessimism serves in the best way their new tastes for expansion. It's not so bad, actually, to be a pessimist—pessimism holds the Golan Heights. It holds the Sinai and the West Bank. It is profitable now to be a pessimist, it is patriotic. . . ."

The American was driven once up to the highlands along Syria that were taken in one of the most celebrated attacks of the 1967 campaign, passing briefly through a small town only a few miles from the Syrian border called Kuneitra, its streets now vacant and still between broken empty houses of stone and plaster. But aside from an occasional Israeli army camp in the trees beside the road, where young soldiers and girls were stretching before their tents in the tender early morning, these altitudes of high windy Swiss-like ridges—blowing with wildflowers, with a ghost of pale mammoth snow-veined mountains in the distances—seemed singularly empty of life, abandoned and voiceless, littered only with incidental manglings of rusted wreckage from those few quick vicious days three years before, left for the most part now to the cumbersome circlings and flappings of solitary storks: "Those are the old fellows who couldn't make the migration to Europe this year," his driver explained. "They are the leftovers staying behind here waiting for winter, when all of them will die." They stopped eventually at one former Syrian fortification on the Golan Heights which had, it seemed, been left carefully untouched since 1967—a place still of singed dirt like black cinder dust and inhabited now in the hot sunlight by a multitude of flies, with the remnants of ruined machinery—tire shreds, the crumpled hulks of Russian half-tracks, scabrous oil drums—still scattered haphazardly over an endless fluttering and nodding of tall wild thistles. But since 1967, the American noticed, there had collected over the grounds, in the trenches and rubbled bunkers, another, discreet, litter—discarded yellow Kodak boxes. And while they were walking along the ridge, a bus wheezed up into the parking area below them, discharging a party of tourists who filtered murmurously up the hill toward them, their cameras quietly snicking.

On the day he was taken to the Canal, when they passed from the pre-'67 boundary of Israel into the occupied territory, it was as if they had crossed an actual physical line of delineation while traveling across the surface of a polychrome printed map —instantly, in a blink, from green fields into scruffy wastes of khaki-colored sand with Bedouins trudging off a certain measured distance from the road, out in a silence and timelessness beyond even the ubiquitous strewn scraps of Egyptian trucks and jeeps. They passed through several villages like mud-dauber nests clustered in the dappling shadows of date palms with goats ambling through their lanes, and then the American realized they were dashing through the city of Gaza: "Roll up the windows, please," muttered the army captain assigned to accompany him on the trip. "Now we drive a little faster, is more healthy," and he snapped open the dashboard compartment and withdrew a cartridge clip which he hurriedly chocked into his machine gun—a pudgy fellow, precipitously polite and congenial, if with a gently distracted and troubled air about him, speckled with sandy freckles, balding and unmarried, and no doubt the woe of some mother somewhere, and, almost as if in acknowledgment of this, obsessively and painfully deferential, self-effacing with constant little light skittering laughs, despite the imposing accouterment of his name: Captain Joshua. Now, passing through a repair gang ranked along the road—Arabs wrapped in kaffiyehs who, engaged in a steady and seemingly profitless scraping, appeared captured by their shovels, dark figures laboring like fitful mute shadows in a sullen black smoke that boiled and billowed from hot tar across the road, staining the bright morning sunlight—Captain Joshua lit another cigarette, which he smoked with quick rapid shallow sips, ashes dusting down over his shirt front. "Ah, Gaza," he said at last, when the city was behind them. "Very tough, yes. Better you don't stop there for coffee, yes," and, fanning the air briefly with his hand, he ducked his head sidewise in another tight little puttering laugh.

They stopped later at a filling station in a glaring and sleazy little seashore city called El Arish, and immediately a numberless conjuration of children clustered at the rolled-up windows of the car. Begrimed and antic, shrilling, they dangled strands of small dyed shells from twiglike hands covered, it seemed, with some yellowish machine oil, as Captain Joshua wheeled with a small wheeze, quickly hammered down the locks on all the doors and then, with a flat little smile pasted on his face, merely sat in the front seat looking straight ahead through the windshield as the imploring grimaces, the soft frenzied scuffling, the thin sibilant bedlam, continued behind the panes of glass around them. After a moment, a light sprinkling of sweat appeared on his upper lip and his forehead. Finally, after they had pulled away and were some distance down the road, he rolled down his window and took out a handkerchief to wipe his face, his neck. "I am, of course, not a regular member of the army," he suddenly blurted. "I am merely in the reserve. Actually, I work in the public relations department of my city's public power plant. But every summer, you see, I have to serve several weeks of active duty. . . ."

Perhaps inevitably, what could be the gravest toll taken on the life of Israel by the occupation has been a gathering contempt for the occupied—the same sort of contempt, curiously enough, in which the Jews themselves were held for so many centuries before 1948. One girl, an immigrant from Schenectady, announced to a dinner table of journalist photographers one evening in Jerusalem, "The Arabs, I don't know why they keep on—they'll never be able to defeat us, because their genes are just different from ours." Of course, there was a certain imported American vigor to her remark, but with a disquieting frequency the American came across similar, if less strenuous, asides from cabdrivers, his escorts from the press and tourist ministries: "We found out about the Arabs in 1967, believe me—one run, all run. Just like bloody cattle. . . ." One Israeli journalist dismissed all prospects of reaching any accommodation with the paranoias and sensitivities of the Arabs with a hiss. "Well, fuck them anyway," he said. "I mean how do you deal with half-deranged adolescents? Why even bother to try?" Riding one morning through an Arab village in an occupied area, the American's driver nodded toward a gallery of Arab men sitting against a white sunlit wall along a dirt lane and whispered, "Just look at them. My God, how they like to sit! I'm telling you, if sitting were a profession, they'd all be rich—" and then later in the afternoon, as they were passing near the Lebanese border, the driver climactically declared with a sweep of his hand, "Across those mountains, of course, live our cousins, the pigs. They are our cousins, yes, but they are pigs,

I must say that." (They had stopped that afternoon at a medical clinic maintained by Israel near an Arab village, and after conducting the American through its waxen halls—leading him briskly into successive rooms filled with a general alarmed flutter of Arab women startled by their abrupt appearance— the driver paused outside to speak to an Arab nurse who, merely glancing at him, strode crisply on by them without replying. The driver gave a small dull laugh: "Ah, you see how they are? Believe me, if there are no other Arabs around, she'll speak to me every time. But if there are Arabs anywhere nearby, you see, she won't say a thing to me. . . .")

Leaving his hotel in Jerusalem one evening, the American discovered, sitting alone and dour on a bench in the lobby like an abandoned teddy bear, Amos Kenan, who glanced up at the American and pronounced abruptly, without preliminaries, "This is a sad city. It is divided without a wall," and im- mediately fell silent again. Indeed, despite Israel's official an- nexation of Jerusalem's Arab quarter, the American found that both Arab and Israeli cabdrivers were still unable to navigate in each other's section of the city, and one Arab driver with whom he rode frequently—a heavy hulking somewhat sulky youth named Ismail—declared before long, "You know I am now Israeli citizen, yes? O.K., but why I cannot go anywhere I want in Israel? Why they stop me, search me all the time? I pay now Israeli taxes—you tell me, mister, why I am treated still as a foreigner. You see green license plate on my cab? That is license they make all Arabs put now on their cars, so when I carry passenger to Tel Aviv, they know I am Arab, drivers shout to me why I do not go to Jordan, want to fight me all the time—" (In fact, early one morning as Ismail was carrying the American to the airport in Tel Aviv, a car pulled up as they were stopped for a red light and the young Israeli behind the wheel, noticing Ismail's license tag, began shouting and gesturing at him. "He wants to know why I am here in Tel Aviv," Ismail interpreted for the American, "he asks where are my papers. I say to him, who is he to question me, I am Israeli citizen. He say then to me, do I want trouble. You see, it is something happening all the time to me in Tel Aviv.") But Ismail asserted, "I don't care who comes—the Jews, the Americans, the Russians—this is my home. I stay here, I have nothing else. But I resist them. You want to know how? See— these Israeli cigarettes, but I buy them from Arab, even if cost double. The same with everything—I buy my eggs Arab, I buy my bread Arab. This is supposed to be democracy—" They were now on a forsaken road outside of Jerusalem, on the way to Bethlehem with nothing around them but a landscape of shadeless rocky hills, and Ismail suddenly blared, "So if I think Dayan sheet, I can say to anybody that Dayan sheet. And that I will say, I say it now—yes! I say it! . . ."

One morning on the way south to the kibbutz in the Negev Desert where the American was to spend a few hours with David Ben-Gurion, Ismail picked up an Arab hitchhiker—a shepherd in his thirties with a sturdy sun-chapped generous face who presently, after a few short questions from Ismail, leaned over into the front seat and began talking with eager flourishes of his blunt thorny hands: "He say that before '67 he could go and come without difficulty," Ismail translated; "he used to bring, how you say, sheep and goats and—yes, livestock, he used to bring livestock from Turkey, Amman, Baghdad, and raise them on his land to sell. He had at one time two hundred heads of animals. But now, he say, it is almost dead in finding work and daily bread. He has now only one lamb, for the fresh milk for his children—nine children he has. So he went to Jerusalem to find work, but he did not know there was this necessity for a piece of paper to go into Jerusalem, because he does not read or write. You cannot enter Jerusalem without permission from high commissioner. So they put him in jail for four days; he just got out this morning. He had to pay two hundred pounds—his family borrowed the money for him. So now he must find something else to do, because they told him not to come back into Jerusalem—" All the while through this recital of disasters, the shepherd maintained an expression of detached simple cheerfulness, as if he were merely recounting mischievous vagaries of the weather over the past week. "His wife, he says, was very sick during the winter, until they finally come and take her away and put her in clinic. They told him she was going to die, so he prepared everything to bury. But Allah left her alive for the sake of the nine children. His brothers gave blood for his wife, because he had no money to buy it. So now, what he is going to do, he will borrow underwear and carry it in a suitcase to the camps and fields and sell it to the peasants. . . ." On the outskirts of Hebron, they stopped to let the shepherd out, and the American suddenly found himself withdrawing from his wallet a random clutch of Israeli pounds, even as he felt himself flushing, a faint burn in the tips of his ears: "How much is this, Ismail?" he asked quickly, and Ismail peered at him, blinking, "You are going to give that to him?" He stared at the ruffle of bills: "You are going to give all that to him?" The American was aware he was grinning blankly, an awry insistent grin fixed helplessly on his face with a small dull ache in his cheeks, and he said, "Just ask him if he will accept it," and Ismail turned and said something to the shepherd, who had already stepped out of the car. After a moment, the shepherd laughed, shaking his head, merely dispensing a short acknowledgment to the American with a flip of his fingertips from his forehead. "He says he thanks you, but he cannot—you are his friend. . . ." And the American said, "Wait a minute, tell him as a favor to me—" even as he was thinking, *But what for? A private American gesture of commiseration and small restitution? But I've done nothing to this man. I am connected in no way to his troubles, or the troubles of any of them over here, actually,* and then he remembered that delicate accusation by candlelight in the hotel dining room a few nights before, the Jewish girl from Morocco abruptly inquiring, "So you will spend a few weeks more here, and then you will return to America, but how can you know? How can you expect to know the suffering that easily, without ever having experienced it even just a little bit yourself?" and he thought, *Maybe then it's just a journalist's fee, some duty paid for having made the passage exempt of the suffering, or, for God's sake, am I going around purchasing portions of people's woe and travail? . . .* At last the shepherd accepted the bills, holding them for a moment with a delicate and uncertain awkwardness before plunging them absently in his coat pocket. A few minutes later, several miles down the road, Ismail abruptly declared, "You know, when he gets into town and tells them you gave him that money, they will not believe him," and then after a long silence, he blurted out, with the slightest shadow of a peevish pout on his face, "The driver of a cab, you know, does not make so much that he could ever give away to someone so many pounds as that. . . ."

Nearing, by midafternoon, Ben-Gurion's kibbutz in the Negev, they passed a tawny stubbled plain across which there moved with an imperceptible progression the distant figures of Bedouins on camels, beyond them the solitary stalkings of high-tension towers. Eventually, this prairie faded into desert, a dust-blown cinnamon wasteland in which Sde Boker—Ben-Gurion's kibbutz—appeared with an abrupt apparitional improbability in the emptiness: a small self-intact geometry of streets, lawns, flower beds, sidewalks, set down with the unreality of some movie set. The American waited for a while in the small house where a kind of palace guard—sober young sabras, with strangely chaste faces—keep watch with UZIs and a two-way radio on Ben-Gurion's quarters across a small grassy yard out their window—an inauspicious low shedlike dwelling where, his wife now dead, having retired himself from the Knesset, he is writing his memoirs. After a few minutes, the American mentioned that he had been in Egypt and Jordan only a few weeks ago, and one of them turned on him a brief glittering gaze, and snapped, "You do not need to explain to us the Arab, I assure you. We know what the Arab is." After a pause, the American casually said that he had ridden down with an Arab driver. The guard's eyes widened momentarily, and then, with a bristle of irritation in his voice, he turned to another man in the room and snapped some instructions; the man quietly got to his feet and left the room. The guard then turned back to the American and said, "We will keep a close eye on him, I assure you of that. You should not have come down with an Arab driver."

Finally the American was shown into Ben-Gurion's quarters— a long low-ceilinged barrackslike room with a linoleum tile floor and green prefab walls, simply and modestly furnished, with a large portrait of Ben-Gurion's wife, a delicate vaporish drawing like a Japanese print, on a far wall. Presently, Ben-

Gurion entered from his office door: a diminutive plug of a man, his small puckered eyes now a bit blearied with his eighty years, the famous unconfined fuming of his hair now thinned and snipped, but still with that terrierlike clamp to his mouth of resolute indomitability, a figure now widowed and solitary whose single life encompasses the whole long labored terrific creation of the state of Israel—who, indeed, even named it. He noticed after a moment that a tape recorder had been placed unobtrusively on the coffee table beside his chair, and he turned to the guard who had ushered in the American, "So what is this," speaking then in Hebrew with a certain crackling gruffness, but the guard, as he muttered an answer, did not look at him, merely bent low over the recorder as he hastily softly furtively threaded the tape and then arranged the mike. Ben-Gurion shrugged: "Well, he says that someone called and told him a tape recorder. So—" He sat on the very edge of his chair, leaning forward with his feet spread and one hand cocked on his knee, a pose yet of some pent urgency and velocity, of earnest exhortation, his feet in bedroom slippers constantly flexing, shuffling back and forth. Wearing a short-sleeve shirt, his bare arms beginning to thin a bit, with the soft pellucid quality of white wax, he suddenly resembled a slightly miniaturized version of the American's own grandfather—the same redoubtable chomp of his lower jaw as he talked, the same way of absently folding one ear forward with the flat palm of his hand, the same white frosting of beard on his jowls, and the same faint clean smell of vanilla of those summer evening hours just before supper. As he talked—"Most of my days, I am alone, writing the whole time, writing things fifty, sixty years ago"— a vague swim of sunlight and leaf shadows wavered on a far wall in the late fading afternoon, and he reminisced in a kind of aimless rummaging through the past half century. The after-noon soon filled with fleeting tatters of laughter and argument and clangorings from that immense long subplot of corridor conferences and rallies and train journeys all over Europe that patiently proceeded beneath the progress of world wars and peace conferences, shadowed the major convolutions of history for fifty years, until it finally availed in Israel in 1948. Now and then, he would seem to trace certain years into some sudden unexpected fog: ". . . In 1939—wait, in 19—19—1933—33," shaking his head briefly, his eyes lightly closed for a moment, and waving his hand fretfully in front of his face: "Ah, I said 1939, but it was, yes, '33—"

His great obsession over that half century, of course, was the ingathering of the Jewish peoples in Palestine, and he would inevitably confront even visiting Jewish American benefactors and fund raisers: "You send money, why don't you come over yourself? Where would America be if the English, the Irish, the Germans had merely sent over their money and stayed home?" Once during the course of the afternoon, he even paused and inquired of the American journalist, "And you— are you Jewish?" But he finally declared, "We are not really a state yet. We must have another five or six million Jews at least. The desert must be settled. Where we are now—this is neither the beginning nor the end. We are in the middle." But, accord-ing to reports in Tel Aviv and Jerusalem, Ben-Gurion had recently been entertaining impatient misgivings about new im-pulses he saw emerging in Israel after the 1967 war, specifically what he considered a growing tendency since the occupation to resort to Arab labor for those elemental barehanded tasks in the country like construction and repair work. But now, with the tape recorder quietly spooling beside him and the guard entering periodically to change the reels, he only allowed, "If it had been up to me, we would have had peace two days after the war. I know the land we had before the Six-Days War was enough for eight million Jews to settle. If it would depend on me, I prefer to live in peace with our neighbors than we should have the territory. If I had to choose between war with the Arabs and only a small part of Israel as it is now, I would give up much of the territory, take only the small part. It's enough."

As they stood at the end of their conversation, Ben-Gurion's head gave a kind of quick benedictory bob: "You know something, I was born a Zionist—it was not until I was fourteen that I became a Socialist and revolutionary. But when I got here, I began more and more to understand the Bible. Now, I will tell you, all my views come from the prophets." The American then asked him with which one of the prophets he felt now—after eighty years of life on this earth, and at this moment in the development of Israel—most intimate, most comfortable. He coughed, and then after a silence, murmured: "Jeremiah. Jeremiah. He was a very unhappy man, you know. . . ."

Earlier in the afternoon, during the long drive down from Jerusalem to the Negev, Ismail at one point had ventured, "Ben-Gurion, he was a very good man. None of them now are like Ben-Gurion; they are different kind of men, but Ben-Gurion was very great. I would like very much to meet him—maybe this afternoon I get the chance, do you think?" So the American now informed Ben-Gurion, "You have an admirer outside, the driver who brought me down here. He happens to be an Arab, but he wanted very much to shake your hand," and Ben-Gurion sputtered, "Of course—of course! He is outside, you say?" They emerged from the house and the American

motioned to Ismail, who was waiting in his car a few yards
away, and Ismail immediately, with a clumsy plunging alacrity,
scrambled out and came striding toward them, a lurching gait
between a formal march and a sprint, tilted slightly off-balance
with a wide grin sprawled across his face, holding one arm
stiffly at his side with a cigarette in his rigid fingers. Instantly,
three guards materialized out of the dusk, two of them collect-
ing around Ben-Gurion and the other approaching the American
to ask in a low even monotone, "What is this? What is the
idea? What does this driver of yours think he is doing?" They
glared with shocked affront as Ismail shook Ben-Gurion's hand,
and then one of them said to Ben-Gurion in a clipped rapid
voice, "You should not be outside in your shirt sleeves, it is
too cool. You must go back—" and Ben-Gurion, slapping his
arms briskly, snorted without looking at them, "No, no, I am all
right, the weather is nice. Stop worrying. . . ." Ismail, his face
studiously sober, announced with a certain momentous gravity,
"Yes, sir, I saw you once in Munich when I was working there
in 1963. You had come for a meeting, a conference of some
sort, I believe. I remember seeing you once then—" and Ben-
Gurion, a momentary vague puzzlement on his face, inquired,
"In 1963? But I don't think I was in Munich in 1963—I don't
remember, but 1963 I don't think I—" Ismail, still standing
with a vaguely formal rigidness, his arms stiffly straight at his
sides and his cigarette now smoldering close to his knuckles,
heartily and cheerfully insisted, "Yes, sir. It was 1963. I was
working in Munich then, and it is something I have always
remembered, I saw you when you—" and suddenly one of the
guards snapped at Ismail, "No. He was not in Munich in 1963.
Now, is there anything else you want to know?" But Ben-
Gurion, ignoring them, continued talking to Ismail, the two of

them exchanging remarks in German and French and then Arabic, until finally Ben-Gurion—a squat and stubby figure standing with his hands shoved deep in the pockets of his baggy trousers, his feet still in slippers—ventured lightly, "And you are from Jerusalem, so now you are an Israeli citizen. So could you also know a little Hebrew, perhaps?" Ismail, with a quick and eager intake of his breath, immediately began speaking to him in Hebrew, somehow like a child proudly performing a mastered facility, and Ben-Gurion nodded briskly with a brief smile. "Very good, very good. I have learned Arabic, you have learned Hebrew. We can talk." But then one of the guards— who all this time had been stalking impatiently and restlessly around the two of them, with repeated glowers at Ismail— abruptly declared again to Ben-Gurion that he should go back inside out of the evening air. Ben-Gurion shook Ismail's hand once more, and turned and padded slowly back into his house while a guard came over to the American again and muttered tonelessly, "Your driver, he is not supposed to be here, you know. I don't understand why you came down with him; it was a very bad idea. If he is stopped on the way back, he will be arrested." The guard then stopped Ismail beside his car and barked, "Did you not know you are not allowed to come here? Where are your papers?" Ismail, his face blank, fumbled out his wallet and produced an array of identification cards, certifications, permission slips, licenses, which the guard hastily perused, shortly shoving the wallet back into Ismail's hand: "Get back to Jerusalem. I don't care what permissions you have, if you are stopped after dark, you will be arrested. . . ."

Once out of the kibbutz, on the highway again, Ismail said in a thick strangely strangled voice, "You see what I tell you? Why they speak to me as if I am a dog? I am citizen from second class. But Ben-Gurion, he is not like the rest of them. If he still the President, it would not be as it is now for the Arabs. . . ." The desert's limitless empty tumbling of rises and ridges was subsiding into shadows around them now like a gradual tremendous sinking into some dark sea, while a pale pearly shine lingered for a moment longer in the sky, the day burning out at last in a long thin dusty red smolder low in the west, and with a few last scattered flares of light on the tips of hills around them, like brief extinguished beacon fires, the landscape sank fully into night. Having to detour around Hebron in the occupied zone now that it was after sundown, Ismail drove through unfamiliar towns, becoming momentarily lost in some of them but not asking directions from anyone on the sidewalks, merely wheeling around corners in a kind of subdued wordless panic until at last he found his direction again. On the outskirts of Gat, they picked up two soldiers hitchhiking at a highway intersection illuminated now in the night with the white brilliance of a magnesium glare—thin youths no more than eighteen, with the fresh frail faces of acolytes, who, after stooping beside the front window to peer in carefully at Ismail as they exchanged a few words in Hebrew with him, got into the back seat where they rode in silence, merely whispering something to each other now and then. At last, Ismail introduced the American as a journalist, announcing they were on their way back from Sde Boker, where they had visited Ben-Gurion that afternoon. With that, one of the youths leaned forward, his two hands lying side by side on the back of the front seat, and began talking to the American in faltering English, his voice quiet and pleasant but earnest, explaining that he planned to study electrical engineering after the army, that neither he nor his friend enjoyed the military but, like all

Israelis, recognized it was a necessity for the time being: "No one is hating the Arab peoples; no one in Israel is wanting to hurt or to kill Arab peoples. No. I am myself having a love for all peoples, all men. The Arabs, they are like us, they are to us brothers. I am wishing to live with Arab peoples in peace. Yes? But the leaders of the Arab peoples, they are telling the Arabs Israel is an enemy to them, Israel wish to kill Arab peoples and to take all the Arab lands away from them for Israel. So the Arab peoples, they are hating Israel and wishing to destroy us. It is not good. I am not wishing to fight them, but there is for us no choice—" The youth then turned to Ismail, who had been listening silently, his face expressionless, and said, "Is not so, you agree?" Ismail answered, his voice somewhat loud, "No—I do not agree." Without moving his eyes from the road, he lifted his head slightly toward the youth and placed his fingertips on his chest: "Because I am Arab." The American saw the youth exchange a quick mute glance with his companion in the dark of the back seat, a briefest dim flicker of eyes in the soft glow from the dashboard. Still leaning across the front seat, but very still now, the youth at last breathed, "Ah. . . ." They rode for a while in a hush. Finally the youth murmured, his voice having faded slightly, "As I am saying, I am having no hate for Arab peoples, because in my heart I know is not good to hate. For you, I have only a feeling of wanting to be a friend. Why can this not be? You are good man, but why are some Arabs wishing to kill Israelis? . . ." "Because," Ismail now boomed, "Israel took their land, drove them away. I am also feeling as all Arabs do—but what can I do? I have family, children—if they find me with bomb, everything is taken away, my family will starve, I am in prison or killed. But I am Arab—you think I not feel the same way?"

The other youth shifted quietly in the back seat and stared out of the window, while his companion, his voice now diminished almost to a whisper, ventured, "But why? You are Israeli citizen now in Jerusalem, so your life is better—" and Ismail fairly blared: "How better? How better? I pay Israeli taxes, but if I leave Jerusalem, I am stopped, searched. You are sabra, I am sabra, too. I am born here, too, but you can go, I cannot go. You are not searched all the time, I am searched. How is this better?" A slight flatness, just an edge of brittleness had now entered into the youth's voice: "These things are because there are some Arabs who are wishing to bomb and make all the time trouble. How they know you do not have bomb or something? These things, they are—what is the word, inconveniences?—inconveniences that are necessary. It is having nothing against you personally—" "Yes," Ismail explained, "but I am citizen, why I do not have the same rights as you? Why I am treated different?" He was growing noticeably more effusive behind the wheel, and finally the American proposed, "Let's not open up another front here in this car. As the American, the third-party neutral here, I hereby declare a truce in this car. All right? We will let the peace begin right here in this car," and as if released from some subtle enpinionment, the youth gave a small laugh and leaned back at last from the front seat. Ismail, however, continued staring straight ahead, his mouth still open in impatient and almost panting indignation. They were passing now a few miles from Tel Aviv, and suddenly the youth's companion turned from the window and said something in Hebrew; the youth then leaned forward again and said, "This is good. We get out here." Ismail snapped, "You want to get out here? O.K.," and brought the car to a slowing savage dusty halt. After the two soldiers got out, before the youth shut the back door again, the American said to him, "Shalom," and the youth leaned in and said to Ismail, "I am wishing for you the best happiness. You are a good man. Someday we will be friends. Shalom—" but Ismail, turning in his seat, merely lifted his hand in the air for a moment and said nothing, a small dry smile on his face.

Release

THE NEXT MORNING—the day the American was to leave, to return home—he awoke into a calm innocent brightness that seemed, in his small staid hotel room, somehow like the grave light in a chapel choir. The idle sounds in the street below came to him now as if from a great distance. As he passed through all the small procedures of departure—eating breakfast for the last time in the hotel's quiet flagstoned low-vaulted dining room, settling his bill, packing his bags with a curious heedless haphazard haste, riding finally from Jerusalem to the airport in Tel Aviv—he had somehow the feeling of a fugitive, was aware of a faintly delirious sensation of escape, a slight breathlessness, an almost painful exhilaration, thinking, *So nothing happened. The passage has been negotiated, and nothing happened after all.* . . . The six weeks at his back already seemed as remote as some complex improbable dream, a Joycean fugue of visions and voices and furies in the deep caverns of a long sleep from which he had awakened only that morning. the endless sunny streets of wreckage in Suez with that florid faded pornographic movie poster fluttering soundlessly from

193

the marquee; quiet distant bumps in the bright noon as the high invisible whine of Israeli jets passed overhead; the Egyptian doctor sitting in the twilight on the lawn at the Gezira Club musing, "Sometimes I get the feeling we just don't belong in this century"; the child that morning at the orphanage outside Amman stirring briefly in her sleep as a bell clanged outside the window, and the sudden surge of those dark figures under a seethe of flags over the sunlit white stones of the amphitheatre; that long night in his hotel room before the commando raid, the tea sipped with some secret ceremoniousness; then, at the fedayeen post in Irbid before they set out for the river, Abdullah smiling shyly and tapping his forehead, "No, I be afraid . . ." and returning later deep into the night to find the looming figure of that nameless knapsacked vagabond revolutionary standing under the shadeless light bulb, *So here he is, the sonnuvvabitch himself—Death;* and Czech, at the kibbutz whose lights he had seen twinkling from the other side of the Jordan that night with the Palestinians, flinching at the sudden thrumming whine of the generator they passed, "I tell them, so be afraid. But don't leave—just don't leave . . ."; and the evening in the living room of the kibbutz leader in Galilee with the rich wistful taste of the brandy and Gregorian chants playing in another room, "You see, for over four thousand years somebody or other has been trying to destroy us . . ."; and the night with the commandos at the deserted moonlit village when he had looked for an instant into that face in the match flame's glare. And the bridge. That morning at the bridge. . . .

Now in his plane, on the runway waiting for the takeoff, the American thought once more, *It was as if all of it were suddenly reduced to that last prisoner they released, that one casualty. Because he had looked full into the face of it. . . .* They had been brought from Amman, a large contingent of foreign journalists in a government press-ministry caravan, to witness the release of prisoners taken by Israel as suspected guerrillas in a raid on an Arab community some two years before. The procession of cars descended out of the high Jordanian hills with chill flavors of fir and cedar in the air, down rubbled rocky chasms with a niggardly bitten agriculture on their slopes, down at last into the Jordan Valley's white dusty glare, where the American could see, in the distant sweep of the valley on the other side of the river, the faint brief stain of green that was Jericho, and beyond that, almost imperceptible in the morning's burnished haze of heat, the far apparitional loom of the Mountains of Moab. They were proceeding now along a thin dirt road past the vacant shadowed doorways of a last Moslem village, a few Arabs and Jordanian soldiers clumped in scraps of shade in the dirt yards, and finally into a region where the last meager trees played out completely into a shadeless glowering flat land mangily tufted with brush and weeds, a leprous desolation of whiteness under a hot pale shimmering sky like galvanized tin, passing down through gullied banks bleak as phosphorus, calcium, scribbled over with barbed wire, until at last they reached the river itself, the bridge where they found a small congregation of trucks and jeeps and Jordanian troops.

Here, for about an hour, they waited, with a trivial chirping of birds in the hot still morning, a continuous quiet sighing of water under the bridge as the Jordan, that fabled river of Biblical battles and epiphanies which he found little more than a deep and sluggish olive-brown creek, eddied deeply past close muffling banks of evergreen. In the shadows of the trees across the plank bridge, the Israeli guards walked back and forth, figures only some fifteen yards away, their faces shadowed under their caps but the tips of ball-point pens discernible in their shirt pockets, yet with that quality of a profound remoteness, as distant as if they were actually in another dimension, another world.

Finally, with a small fitful fanfare of beeping and flags fluttering from fenders, the Red Cross cars and trucks arrived on the other side, and after a short consultation between Israeli and Jordanian officers in the center of the bridge, the prisoners began crossing over—one by one, each of them carrying their belongings in white bags supplied by the Red Cross, which gave them the look of passengers disembarking with their meager baggage at a small-town bus terminal, their faces with the wan sodden pallor of convalescents in the sun, vacant and vaguely bewildered as if unable to realize, to assimilate after three years, such spaces around them again, much less the fact they were free. Once they reached the other side of the bridge, they were engulfed by the waiting crowd in embraces, slaps on the back, in the midst of which they remained oddly passive, withdrawn, until they were led on to the antique bus, painted a mint green with a salmon-colored stripe, where the others were sitting looking quietly out of the windows.

Then, after a pause, a brief exchange of whispers and papers, the last prisoner was brought forward. Slumped on the arm of a cellmate, he was led onto the bridge, his feet shuffling, his head swinging slowly and dully and steadily from side to side, swallowing deeply with a repeating convulsiveness, his mustache dewed with spittle, an oblivious stare on his face. There was a hush now in the morning on both sides of the bridge; the Israeli officers stood off to one side with a subdued and sober muteness momentarily settled over them as they watched the Jordanian officers go through the brief procedure of checking

196

the man's name on their list. He waited on the arm of his companion totally insensate of this transaction of his freedom— a human blank, the American was informed now, deaf and dumb and blind, his mind blasted as empty as that glaring landscape around them all, no voices or movement or meaning of the business now of his release reaching his white pure soundless timeless peace. He merely swung his head softly and continuously back and forth like some last brute gesture of negation, repudiation, absolute and elegiac.

Because he could just as well have been passing across from the other side. Indeed, the American had seen documents detailing what had befallen Israeli pilots captured by the Syrians —men, like this one, returned as idiots. An Israeli intelligence officer had said with a sigh one afternoon, "And if our people happen to fall into the hands of villagers or farmers over there, you know, after what they've been hearing from Radio Cairo and Radio Baghdad for all these years, it's a simple prompt matter of knives and scythes. There is no problem of release negotiations involved in those cases." The Israelis later relayed to the American a Red Cross report on the last prisoner at the bridge, taken from interviews with Israeli prison doctors, which ascribed his condition somewhat dubiously to self-inflicted wounds, with "NOT FOR PUBLICATION" stamped at the bottom of the paper. Of course, he could just as probably have been injured during the fighting itself before he was captured. But it didn't matter. Though the occasion had been contrived by the Jordanians as a polemical event, that last prisoner to cross the bridge, the American knew, was meaningless as propaganda. Because, finally, for him there were no longer any sides made up of ancient national legitimacies or irreconcilabilities. Beyond any mutual political arithmetics of suffering or tabulations of brutalities, he seemed now to the American a casualty of something larger—something brooding over all the paranoias and grievances he had seen in these lands that was as old and tragic as man's career on the earth itself. And the American thought, *He, at least, has looked full into the face of it.* . . .

Led on to an ambulance, the man sat on a cot in the back with the doors still open disclosing him, leaning forward with his hands on his knees and swallowing in the heat, until finally a glass of water was passed unsteadily and splashing from hand to hand over the heads of the crowd, his companion taking it and lifting it to the man's lips, the man accepting it seemingly without notice even, his hands still lying on his knees. Flash bulbs were stammering over him, in a general uproar of shouts. Finally the American found a Jordanian officer and said, "Maybe you should get him on out of here. While they're all taking his picture, he could expire, you know." The officer, his face flushed, his eyes a bit glazed, answered in a high thin eager voice, "Yes. Yes, of course. But you see, his health is the most solid evidence of what the Israelis—" and the American replied, vaguely aware he was shouting now, "Yes, and while you're demonstrating him, he could die on you. . . ."

The next day, an Al Fatah escort conducted the American, along with a television crew, to the hospital where the man had been taken. They found him lying in pajamas straight on his back atop a chintz bedspread, on a simple cot with a pipe-frame enameled in white. His comrade, standing in front of the cot, began narrating an account of what had been done to them both, once pulling up the shirt of the man's pajamas to reveal symmetrically notched scars on his stomach as the cameras were hefted clumsily for closer angles of scrutiny. As the interview proceeded with cords and cables pooled over the floor, the man lying inert in the fitful artificial brilliance of swooping television lights, the American looked out of the window—it was a cool hushed overcast afternoon, autumnal, with some quality in it of benediction and quiescence, the tops of the cedars and firs outside the window softly stirring in the blowing of a chill wind, over an empty and voiceless courtyard. Then the American glanced back at the figure of the man on the bed: with voices still flurrying around him in the room, he lay motionless on his back, gazing blankly at the ceiling, with a sudden glimmering of tears in his eyes.